A Winner's DNA:

Why some people work less and make more than you!

By: Jesper Qvist

Library of Congress Cataloging-in-Publication Data:
Qvist, Jesper

ISBN 10: 0983897204
ISBN 13: 9780983897200

Printed in The United States of America.

First Revised Edition

"If you don't see yourself as a winner, then you cannot perform as a winner."

- Zig Ziglar

Content

Preface

"Great leaders are not born, they are made."

-   William A. Cohen

As the quote by William A. Cohen states above, your winner's DNA is not depended genetically on the way you shape your future. It is rather depended on the way you shape it! A Winner is not born with the genetics of a winner's DNA, but he or she shapes their DNA during their life, which ultimately is making them a winner. A winner knows how to utilize and create winning concepts, ideas, companies, books, applications, and services for other people. They have a talent for working hard in order to achieve their goals, and when people observe them, it seems like it is a gifted talent. A winner is not just a regular person, but also part of a new category of entrepreneurs. I decided to write this book to pass on the experiences from my two masters degrees and my entrepreneurial endeavors, but also to guide you on to find your inner winner. I find it extremely important for people to understand why social media, crowdsourcing, outsourcing, and other tools play such an important role in business life today. People who want to achieve status as a winner need to know how to use these tools, and when they do so, they will create even more value than they never thought was possible.

- Jesper Qvist, Miami – August 2011

Part 1

What is a Winner?

What is a winner? That is an intriguing question, since people often have different answers to it. Society is so diverse and so multicultural that a vast array of individuals influences us. Though this is true in the world we live in today, one thing the majority of people have in common is that a winner is often linked with success, which is often related to social status and money. Most people look at success and money as the ultimate goal, which in reality, most might never accomplish or attain. Many people work for years in dead boring jobs, hoping to get the promotion that gives them the status of a Winner one day and makes their dreams come true. The problem is that these people often sit there in the corporate world wishing and hoping for a miracle to come around. They would often look at famous entrepreneurs such as Mark Zuckerberg, the founders of Google, Bill Gates and other extraordinarily rich and successful people, and wish they were like them. But the truth is that these guys worked hard, and they were willing to risk it all—and in doing so they did in fact all become billionaires.

This book is written to identify the traits of successful people, identify tools and business models that would help you advance to become a successful entrepreneur and quickly join the list of winners, which is closer than you think.

If you pay attention to many of the people around you, you might have a friend or have met a person who travels the world all the time, and it seems like this person does not work that hard. This person has a lavish lifestyle that you are jealous of and might dream about. The fact is that it is achievable; this person might just be a little smarter at having the right people around him or her. For example, they might have virtual assistants in Asia working for them while they sleep, so they are actually productive 24/7 without being there in person. They might use crowdsourcing as a tool to gather information and ideas from groups of people from around the globe to help build their ideas. They are willing to take on challenges, which awarded them with the lifestyle and title of a winner.

Winners are often inspiring personalities with great drive, and they often have more energy than others. This is due to the fact that they created a lifestyle that is more exciting than most other people would experience. Winners enjoy their freedom and they use it to gather inspiration from their environment, which utilizes their creativity. Most people tend to work too many hours, and research shows that concentration cannot foster satisfactory results when doing so. Winning is not all about hard work, but about doing things right and spending your time and effort on what is important, all with the ultimate goal in sight to become a member of the winning lifestyle.

So this all seems like a great life: to have money and freedom, to travel the world, and to have people admire you and look up to you. If that's your dream, you've decided to open the right book.

A Winners DNA is written from my knowledge and research from real life. I have decided to pass on tools, ideas and methodologies that, if you listen and apply carefully, could change your life to become a winner on first class. Not everybody has the same goals and purpose in life as a winner does. For some the goal and purpose in life is to have a family, a house, and a new car every 3 years; for others it is to create a lavish lifestyle that is more glamorous and free.

10 Things Winners Do Differently

"It always seems impossible until it's done."

- Nelson Mandela, former President

1. *Winners get things done:*

Are you the type that starts a lot of projects due to a dream of joining the club of winners and do not finish them?

A lot of people make a common mistake: they tend to start a project and then lose focus, quickly jumping onto another project. I tried it in my life on several occasions: you start a project then during the process, of completing you come up with something else more exciting, and then it ends up going around in a circle, where you never accomplish anything. Winners have a significant tendency to remain focused when they start something, remaining on top of things where they can have a vision of the project. A winner will manage to finish a project and inspire others to join, in order to make it even better. A winner is often the one that can spot talent and make sure to keep it going. Think about your daily life and what motivates you. Is someone making you go the extra mile without asking, just because they inspire you to do so? Likewise, would you be able to inspire others to go that extra mile for you? If not, then start thinking in terms on how you can inspire others to help you achieve your set of goals.

2. *Winners know how to focus on what you will do, not what you won't do:*

Think about smokers. They often think about how awful it is to smoke, yet 3 seconds later they would light up a cigarette and blame it on addiction. Research shows that you are more likely to quit smoking if you just focus on *quitting*, not *why* you should quit. This is true in business as well: don't focus on what can go wrong or how your competitors might react. If something goes wrong, so be it, and if they react there might not be much to do, but reshaping your idea and make it better is what a winner would do! A Winner will focus on the project itself and look at it as, "how do I get people to love it as much as me? Can I listen and learn from people around me in order to make the product better?"

If you don't focus right today, you should change your ways, ask yourself, what will I do instead in any given situation? For example, if you are trying to gain control of your temper and screaming or even show anger towards others, you might make a plan like "If I am starting to feel or just get close to become angry, then I should take a deep breaths until I calm down." By using deep breaths as a replacement for giving in to your anger, your bad habit will get worn away over time until it disappears entirely.

3. *Winners focus on getting better and better, rather than just being good:*

Believing in your self is essential, and having the ability to reach your goals is significant—but so too is believing you can *acquire* necessary abilities. Many of us tend to believe that our personality, culture, intelligence, and physical aptitudes are fixed. Such people believe that these factors cannot be changed, that no matter what they do they would not improve. As a result, they tend to focus on goals that are all about proving themselves to others, rather than developing and acquiring new skills that would give them an edge.

The exciting news—which is fortunate for most of us—is the fact that decades of research suggest that the belief in fixed ability is utterly wrong! Abilities of all kinds are profoundly malleable.

People should realize that change is in fact good and they can change if they wish to do so. Often winners will see the potential in learning something new and challenging themselves, and they actually find it to be an enjoyable journey getting to the destination.

4. Winners don't believe in fate, they decide to create their own destiny!

Many people tend to use "fate" or "bad luck" as the excuse for their mishaps. Luck is noteworthy, but one does not become lucky if they do not change, believe and keep trying. Winners that do get things done, but take on more projects than others is tempting fate and start to get into the spiral of *"not getting things done."* If you take on too many tasks or projects you are not creating destiny but actually tempting fate to make you lose. The best option is to be realistic and create your own destiny, get things done, and not believe that fate is playing a trick on you; luck, instead, is complementary for the one who is trying.

5. Winners are realistic and optimistic!

We all have a friend (or friends) that believes he or she can build a Dotcom company overnight to instantly become another lucky billionaire and live happily ever after like in a fairytale. Well, the truth is that in reality Rome was not built in one day, nor were any great companies you've ever heard of. Facebook and its creator Mark Zuckerberg took some years to gain million of users and a market value of +$1 billion; Microsoft is the same story, and the list can go on and on. The thing with these types of companies is that the leaders did not intentionally start with the goal of becoming billionaires, but rather from genuine interest and a realistic goal. Dreams are great, but being realistic is just as important to the creation of any company. I am a firm believer that any industry can be "shaken up" by a startup and by someone with the right idea, but being realistic is what gets that person there. Look at Skype: a Danish and a Swedish entrepreneur were "crazy" enough to revolutionize and disrupt the telecom industry. When they went out pitching their idea to venture capitalists, they were continually turned down, until they met a Danish angel investor Morten Lund who took a loan and funded them. The moral of the story is that the founders knew it was realistic; their vision was just different from others, since they would create a disruption in an existing market but as you might know, they ended up becoming billionaires with Skype.

6. Winners know when to quit:

Many people are afraid of the unknown and they fear quitting in any given situation. Quitting is for many equal to failure, and most people fear a failure above all else. But winners *do* fail, and that is often what brought them back on track and gave them the experience to stop in cases where others would keep losing. Imagine you start investing in a project, and after putting thousands of dollars into the project you come to the realization that it will never work. Most people might stare into the sky and keep putting money into the project because they already spent some money, so why not spend more? But people should be willing to say I am quitting it, and I take my loss; that is truly what makes the difference between a regular person and a winner.

7. Winners have a vision for the future:

Most winners are visionaries, and their vision is often the reason why they started their companies—it is what leads them through tough times, as well. An example, of a public visionary is Steve Jobs that has led Apple to the extraordinary success that it has developed and acquired since Jobs's return. Winners have the instinct of vision, and they can see how the future can be shaped if they believe highly in themselves. You can bring in tools and techniques to become a better visionary if you utilize the information you receive from your surroundings. People often do not realize the power of crowdsourcing and the knowledge of a crowd the people can bring to a company or a person, if they know how to attract the channels. Visionaries are the ones that often see and build upon knowledge collected from others.

8. Winners are specific:

Winners often know how to be specific: they will often say, "*I will lose 5 pounds over the next month*" rather than, "*I will lose some weight.*" Being specific and setting up realistic goals—and then accomplishing them without question—is crucial. What would you prefer: to set a goal that is too high and reach it partially, or to set a goal that is so low that when you reach it you ask yourself, "what now?"

Winners know how to raise the bar and be specific to themselves and the people around them. Famous management guru from India and Harvard Business School (Professor in leadership) —Ram Charan once told me at a conference in Copenhagen for business leaders: "What differ an *effective leader from the rest is the fact that they are specific and get things done. It all starts from the basics of finishing each meeting, even if it takes 10 minutes longer, and they tend to always be specific and finish what they started".* His point is clear: highly effective people tend to get more done than regular people. Small changes in your daily life can make you more specific and effective – which are traits of a winner.

9. Winners seek first to understand, then to be understood:

Winners tend to use empathetic listening, which is genuinely giving others focus and attention, which compels them to reciprocate and have an open mind to being influenced. This creates an atmosphere of care, respect, and positive problem solving. All this simply means that when you listen to others and understand their problems or needs, you will always focus on solving their problems. When you understand them, it always makes it easier to communicate the solution to their needs or problems later. Winners understand how to learn and give back to others. They see opportunities where others see obstacles, and everything is to be changed and improved in their minds.

10. Winners they do win!

Winners do win: that's why they are called winners! In the sport's world, there is only one winner of a given game or match. No one win, silver in a final, they loose the gold medal. In the business world is the answer the same: if you win you most likely got a competitor out of business, and you could expect them to either give up or train harder to get back on you. Winning is for some people a must, but when you have won too much, you might tend to become a sleeping elephant, which was the case for Dell when HP came and took over its position as the biggest producer of PCs in the world. Nokia found the same problem: winning for a too long time and becoming a sleeping elephant and allowing Google and Apple to take advantage of a booming smartphone market.

Does Talent Really Exist?

Talent is overrated, and there are many reasons for such a claim. I believe intelligence and hard work is what creates a talent. Talent has been talked about for ages, and everybody believes that someone is born with a gift. Take Wolfgang Mozart as an example: he could at an early age play piano in ways that no one else had ever seen before. People often stick to the belief that he was born with a gift, and that it was meant to be that he became one of the greatest composers in classical music ever in history. The thing is that Mozart practiced intensely and frequently, which gave him over ten thousand hours of practice at a very early age. Ten thousand hours is, according to several authors and researchers, the magic number for talents to stick apart from others. Other researchers claim that it is not the IQ level either that creates talents such as Tiger Woods, Mozart, Edison, and Einstein but rather the intense training and focus that they got in their specialization. What they realized is that you cannot be the best at everything, but rather become the best at one thing, which often becomes an obsession down the road.

When people watched Tiger Woods or Mozart becoming so gifted or talented in such an early age, it is proven that it is not due to a born gift, that many believes, but actually the amount of intense training. One example is when Tiger Woods attended Stanford University, it was not uncommon that he practiced more hours than anyone else. One time, the coach walked out to the driving range on a stormy and rainy day to find Tiger practicing. The coach was highly surprised and asked Tiger, *"What are you doing out here in such bad weather?"* He replied very casually, *"I am practicing for the British Open, which I am planning to win one day."* The British Open, or *"The Open,"* is famous for tough weather and is considered the biggest golf tournament that a golf player can win. The mindset was what made him able to practice hard enough, and he believed that he would get there one day and accomplish the ultimate goal that he had set for himself at an early age.

Interesting enough, in Silicon Valley is the war for talent, truly a fascinating topic. Facebook, Google, and Apple are all fighting for the brightest and the smartest "talents" that they claim exist in "the Valley." When you look at the personalities in music, sports, and science, their skills are often acquired from extensive training. This means that when Silicon Valley companies pay millions of dollars for a company basically without a product, which is often due to the fact that these people that they are acquiring have a talent. They often make a proud statement that they bought the company for its talent and not its products. These people have acquired their talent over a long time, and this creates a unique fit for the organization.

High-performing businesspeople tend to have incredible memories and seemingly prodigious intellects, but where does all the talent really comes from?

Often these people just work harder than others, and in this way they reach a level of performance that makes them seem more gifted than their colleagues. These individuals often focus on training their memories to easily retain information. Furthermore, they manage to teach themselves techniques for synthesizing the information they have acquired. Research shows that these techniques, when practiced over and over again, amount to essentially the same type of deliberate practice that exceptional people execute in almost every other avenue of life.

Why do winners seem to make their work look easy? The answer is pretty clear: they have mastered how to obtain and retain information they've acquired on a daily basis, and they now how to spot talent and highly effective people who can help them!

One technique that helps people to become better talents without spending over ten thousand hours of practicing is the term "deliberate practice". Deliberate practice is designed to improve your performance in a specific manner. The training can and should be repeated frequently to gain a higher effect on your outcome.

One thing that has inspired me—and is actually a fun way to stay sharp—is Sudoku, which is a game involving patterns and sequences. Exercise your mind by solving one Sudoku puzzle each morning; you will feel much sharper and you will become much more productive down the road. Another way of looking into deliberate practice is examining the way Tiger Woods was practicing. He would take all aspects of his golf swing, and keep practicing one movement in the swing to improve the overall performance. Tiger knew it was necessary to master the game better than anyone else, by doing these types of "boring" exercises.

Getting through practices in the sports world is often all about being around inspiring people who pushes you. That is why mentorship is often extremely important and adapted in the business world. Having a mentor or an entrepreneurial idol that you look up too is very important, and often what gives you the nudge to become a winner.

Part 2

The World has Changed!

"Winning the peace is harder than winning the war."

- Xavier Becerra

The way we do business has changed greatly over the years since the dotcom boom occurred in 2000. The terminology of new concepts such as Social Media, Search Engine Optimization (SEO), Cost Per Mile (CPM), Cost Per Click (CPC), Analytics, Disruption, Crowdsourcing, Outsourcing and many others have become a part of everyday business life. Business models and the way we use measurements, marketing channels and even where people work from have changed. In the past, opening a business was all about a great idea, or about making some kind of service or outlet for the neighborhood stores. Today that picture has changed rapidly, and new channels, services, and mindsets need to be understood and assessed. We live in a free world where technology has enabled us to do work from many places, and that is exactly what winners often know how to utilize. They travel more than others, but they use their trips to gain inspiration, and during the trip they would be connected to all their data, which allows them to become decision makers at any time and place. Availability is really the key in a rapidly changing world.

Winners know how to use technology to create advantages for themselves. Technology, if used the right way, really creates an edge for more people than ever before. Management used to have problems with their customer relationship management systems (CRM), but Salesforce.com figured out how to create a cloud-based solution that was scalable for small business and large enterprises alike. Salesforce's software allowed companies to let their salespeople be on the go, update orders immediately, find information on meetings, and basically have all necessary information in their smartphones. This made the job easier for not only the salesperson but also the internal control at companies, who would now have knowledge about sales data, whereabouts, and actual orders and leads in real time. Salesforce got it right, and many people realized the benefits, which saved companies money and created more winners.

Real-time data and technology use in all aspects of your life creates more freedom and automation of boring tasks than you ever could imagine. Shoeboxed.com and Expensify.com, for example, scan all your receipts for you if you mail them in, or you can do it yourself with a snapshot from your smartphone. When you simply upload a picture of the receipt or business card, and then you actually store it automatically in the cloud, and you have the availability to export it to your accounting program, saving the time it would take doing boring bookkeeping. Tradeshift.com is a free invoicing platform that connects businesses, and Xero.com is the leading accounting system in the cloud, which means that you do it all online. If you combine these services, you can pretty much automate the whole accounting/bookkeeping part of your business, and scale it to become less salary heavy and time consuming. Small technological frameworks like these are truly what separate a winner from the regular people. They understand how to get more for their money and spend less time on time-consuming tasks.

The New Business Landscape!

Social media and why it is important:

Many people believe that social media is one of the most effective marketing channels in the new world. The truth is that if you figure out how to use social media, it can become a great tool for many reasons—but if not, you can end up using money on something that could have been better spent elsewhere. Winners understand social media and they know that through its use they will be able to learn a lot from their customers, which they can use to gain an edge over their competitors. Social media also allows for a direct interaction with customers, which is customer care. Consumers expect companies to react on social media complaints against companies, but they also expect companies to give them credit when they advertise and bring in the word-of-mouth effect about a brand, service or product. Social networks and channels are different, depending on the demographics and geography that you target.

Facebook:

In less than seven years, Facebook has managed to gain more than 750 million users, which makes them the biggest social media network on the planet. Facebook has more members than the United States or the European Union have residents (Facebook.com, 2011). Facebook has a large advantage from its strong user base and the amount of time users are spending on their platform—which has made it the online platform people spend the most time using on average (Comcast, 2011). The unique thing about Facebook is that companies can access users easily through a social acquisition, and when people spread something by word-to-mouth it is strongly effective on the platform.

Twitter:

Twitter, in its recent years, has become extremely popular— especially in the U.S.—and has become the network for breaking news, such as when the revolution in Egypt happened recently a lot of people about it through Twitter. In March 2011, Twitter reached its milestone of 200 million users (Twitter, 2011). Twitter is a different social network than others since everything is limited to 140 characters or fewer. Twitter is another tool that can utilize and/or conduct information from users to engage in crowdsourcing.

Google+:

Google+ is the newest platform in the social media scene, and is maybe one of the most ambitious launches from Google in their history. A famous Silicon Valley venture capitalist, Bill Gross, announced on his Twitter stream that he believes that Google+ would be the fastest growing network to reach 100 million users. Google+ is relatively new since it is not open for the public yet, since it is operating by invitation only at this stage. Google+ could become very important for companies in the future, since the platform is also depending on people's search habits, and is recommending in search results what your network likes, which would potentially influence data collecting from different groups of the future.

Vkontakte (Russia)

Vkontakte is Russia's biggest social media network, with a user base of 135 million as of February 2011. Vkontakte is a very powerful tool to collect information from the old USSR countries, and since Russia is a part of the *"BRIC"* countries, the network's growth is expected to continue to increase over time. Reaching the Russian population when addressing their demographic and their culture is important, but like any other network, Vkontakte losing users to Facebook.

Orkut (South American, part of Google)

Orkut is the biggest social media network of Latin America, but like Vkontakte they are losing members to Facebook. Orkut has around 100 Million active members and Google owns them, so it would be no big surprise if Orkut is later integrated into Google+, and that might be a strong reason for them to stay in business against Facebook.

Tencent (China)

Tencent is the second-biggest social media network in the world, after Facebook, and most people in the western countries might never have heard about the site. Tencent, as December 2010, had more than 640 million members, making it at one point bigger than Facebook. Tencent is the biggest social network in Asia and the best connection to the crowd in that part of the world. It is a publicly traded company, and it really focuses on being the number one social network in Mainland China. Facebook is rumored to make a partnership with Baidu, the Chinese version of Google, to enter the market and compete against Tencent.

When engaging in social media, it is important to target the right network and the ones that are suitable for your business. Are you in music? Then Myspace is still one of the networks you would wish to use. If you were targeting China, you might want to consider Tencent, and for Russia Vkontakte. But picking the right network and figuring out a winning strategy is essential. A great example of one company that did well with social media is Virgin America: the company become notorious for its engagement with their customers through social media, and is one of the most responsive to customer's requests or complaints through Twitter and Facebook at this point.

Search Engine Optimization (SEO)

SEO is probably the cheapest and most important source of advertising and lead generation that a company can invest in. It is pretty simple: when people do searches on Google, Yahoo, or Bing, they often click on the three first links that come up or something that sounds about right on the landing page of their search. If your business is located on page 27, the odds that you receive a lot of clicks from the search engines are close to zero. That means that you have to invest heavily in advertising to gain leads to your website. But imagine you run a business and you invested in SEO, which gave you a top-three ranking on the search engines; that would create far more value than anything else, since you will attract more people than your competition does. So how do you start optimizing your company through SEO?

First you need to figure out what gives you a better ranking, since Google, Yahoo, and Bing's robots search and index from different parameters, so you need to understand those to make more money. You need to make sure that on the following is true of your website:

- You have lots of content.
- You update the content or add new material often.
- That content is generally of high quality, and uses the keywords that you wish people use in search results.
- The content can easily be organized and categorized.

The above is the general assumption, but the fact is that a search engine thinks differently:

1. Quality of content and relevance
2. Remember that Text is Text
3. Write descriptive articles about your data
4. Make sure you use tags on your webpage
5. Tag the headings and make them descriptive

These are examples of how a search engine thinks in terms of context, and also an indicator of your ranking. Search engines furthermore need a lot of sites linking to your site, so a good hint is Wikipedia, since they are ranked high; create a Wiki for your company, and link from Wikipedia to your website to boost your ranking. The tips and tricks are many, but remember that search engines change all the time, and with Google+ your searches will be influenced by your Circles (friends) as well. So my tip is to pay attention to SEO if you want to attract more business, and either hire a professional to help you on a freelance basis or learn more about it on your own.

Analytics

I remember from my MBA, Master of Science, Bachelor and High School how boring statistics seemed, especially when we learned about regression, standard deviations, etc. Today I see it in a different perspective; analytics is really the key to improving your business and heightening sales.

Analytics has changed, and online you can track anything. You can gain data from the second a user enters your site, to when they click, what they click on, and where people often leave, as well as what products and information they read the most. Data like this is key in any decision making for a business, and consumer behavior on websites is extremely important. I know examples of companies that sell software as a service (SaaS), and they changed the standard signup package from free to one that requires a small monthly fee, and most people actually paid without thinking about it; it is incredible that you can by changing a button create so much more value. Another thing is on travel website, when you book a vacation they always by default add travel insurance ranging from 9-30 USD, and often you don't realize that you are buying this insurance, but it is actually just pure profit that they create.

Mailchimp.com is a great tool for sending out newsletters, and what surprised me the first time I used it was that I could actually see who opened the newsletter and where they were from. So if I wanted to take advantage of it, I could see who did not open the mail and actually call them by phone to give them the offer and sale that I emailed about.

Heatmaps is another great tool, which shows where people often click the most on your webpage. Crazyegg.com is a great tool to track your visitors: if you realize they click on the left top corner of your site the most, and you want them to click another place—say, a link to a contest—you might consider moving the contest to these spots that you can see on the heat map.

Browser compatibility is important to check. A friend of mine opened Google Analytics to check the revenue generated from his e-store and he decided to check it for each browser, so that Google would show the revenue per browser used. He quickly realized that people using the browser Opera didn't generate any revenue, so he tested it and realized that people couldn't finish their purchase due to incompatibility. So he decided to fix the issue by hiring a programmer for 30 minutes, and now the Opera users generate revenue as well. This shows you that analytics and small test's can create real value for your business.

Applying all these tools as mentioned, from using social media to gaining insight and spreading your business, is one way to become a winner. SEO is probably the cheapest form for optimization and advertising you can invest in for yourself and your business. Tracking and analyzing your customers and visitors is another example of the professional. Finally, strategizing and working hard doesn't mean that you need to master all these topics, but knowing them and hiring the right people is what really matters, and in the end of the day that is what creates a winner!

Part 3

Be Different!

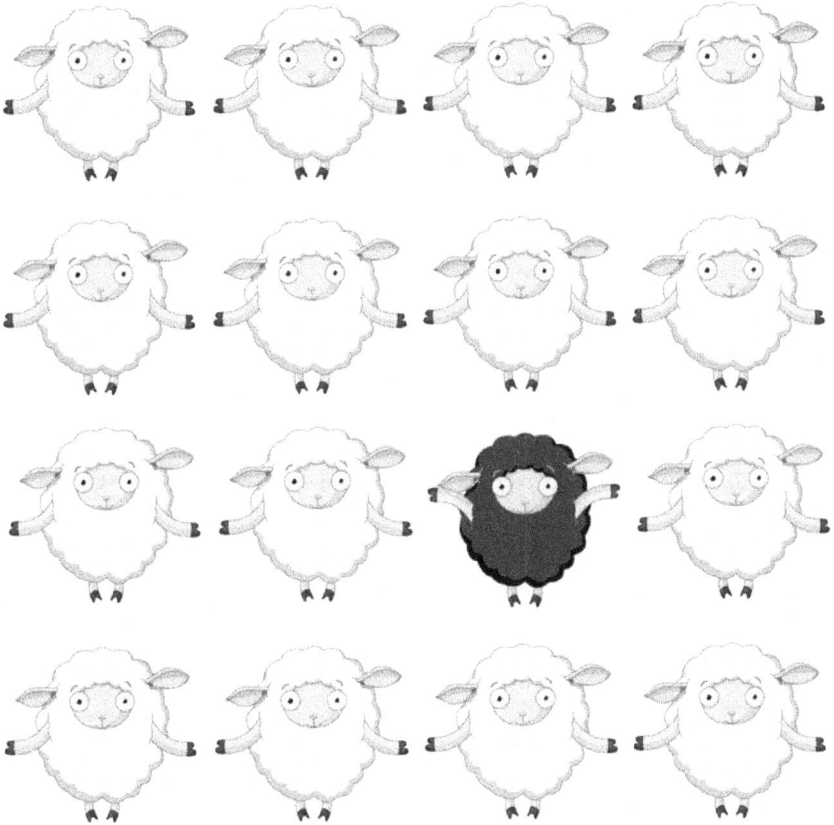

Winners often see the world from a different perspective than others do. Winners tend to believe in change, they believe that doing things in a new and different way could change the way we are, and they create the outmost value of all. Like these sheeps, the black one immediately stands out, and the simple reason is that it is different. The same happened in H.C. Andersen's novel about the ugly duckling: he stood out from the herd at first, but later the other ducks noticed him and he became not just different but remarkable.

Different is what make things remarkable. Remarkable is not just a great way to describe something; it also means that we've found something amazing and it is worth making a remark about. Winners tend to be remarkable and do remarkable things.

When doing remarkable things, winners know that things can become talked about, hyped, and made widely popular by using the right product channels. A great example is how Apple has created a remarkable culture: Steve Jobs is probably the only CEO and marketer that can engage millions of customers in his two-hour long commercials (or as Apple calls them, Keynotes). Imagine having a product where your customers listen to your sales pitch for two hours and later tell all their friends? Winners understand that it is all about engaging the innovators and early adopters when introducing new products. The reason is simple: the diffusion curves have shifted to the left. Not long ago, all marketers aimed to reach the mass market, which is known as the early- and late majority, but today the best way is to be at the fringes, able to access the innovators and early adopters, since they are the messengers to the other consumers, and thus the ones that really matter in all essences of business.

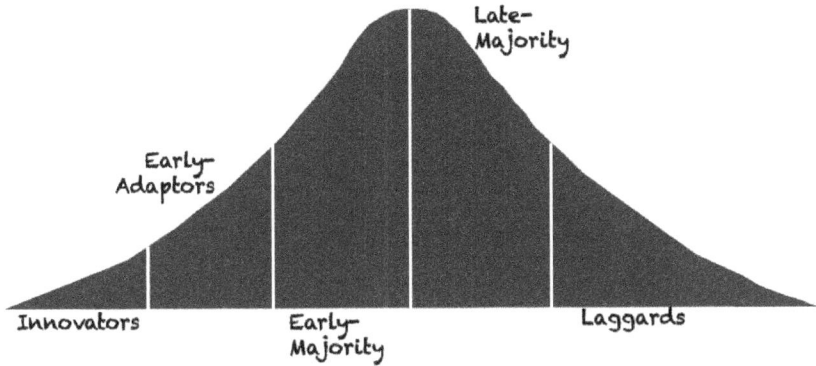

Illustrated above is how a normal diffusion curve looks for new products, but since the world has changed this is how the new version would look like:

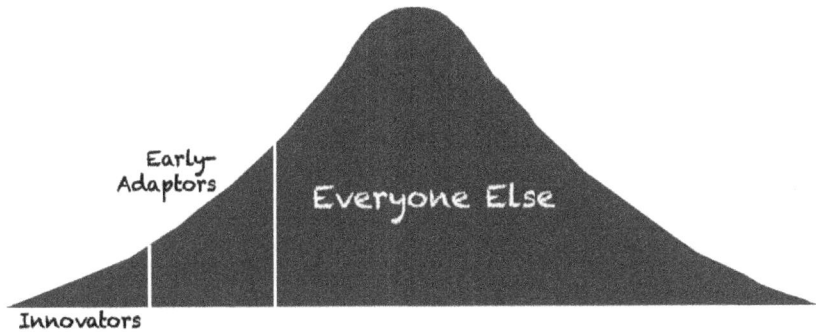

Diffusion is highly connected to a product's level of remarkableness. If you make the same product as everyone else, the odds that people will start buying it are very low. For example, competitors are trying to copy Apple's iPad, and looking at the sales numbers, Blackberry's Playbook is not doing well at all. Why? Quite simply, their product is not different, not remarkable, so why would consumers settle for less and buy something that creates less value for them?

Winners tend to figure out how to turn things upside down. They know when they've figured out how to create remarkableness, and therefore value, for their clients and potential customers. They realize the potential and the power of the crowd and surroundings around their business, and at the end of the day it is a part of the ingredient of becoming a winner!

Be Ubiquitous!

A winner tends to be "ubiquitous," one of my favorite words. The reason why is that you are always present, updated, and to be found everywhere. Being ubiquitous makes people tend to believe that you are everywhere and know everything, when in fact you are not everywhere, but rather just using technology to make it happen. Winners tend to be everywhere, and the ones I know travel around the world and explore it. The thing is many people think they cannot be ubiquitous when they are traveling, which is not entirely true. Often, they understand the importance of being updated with their world, and in fact do some work wherever they are. Imagine you take a trip and travel to hot spots, and let's say one day you email back to a business partner and quote, "Sorry for the delay, I am currently in Ibiza." The next time you speak with him, you might be in St. Tropez, LA, NYC, London, etc. Small answers while being on vacation or just purely traveling make people feel that you are extremely ubiquitous. But most people would ask themselves, why would I be ubiquitous and spend time on a vacation, when I could do something else?

Well first of all, planning and scheduling your online presence upfront can actually do most of the work pre-departure and make people think you work around the clock. Ubiquity is of course a major marketing goal for you and your organization: if you are available you are more likely to gain new opportunities or sustain existing business, and that is why you do it in the first place. There are three main strategies on how to be ubiquitous:

1. *Schedule your social media presence in advance.*

As you know, social media networks never sleep, and neither does the blogosphere. People would look at you as less ubiquitous if you do not regularly update your Twitter feed, Blog and any other channels you might engage in. Often, consistency is key if you are trying to build a strong individual brand or a corporate brand. Remember that there are tools out there, and if you plan updates and write them in advance, you can plan publishing times for the future by using tools such as Tumblr.com, Wordpress.com for your blog, Hootsuite.com and Tweetdeck.com for Twitter, just to mention a few.

2. *Tend to response, when necessary.*

There are many cases where you want to be ubiquitous but you don't have the opportunity. Hiring virtual assistants is one solution. Developing filters and systems to prioritize emails and information is a second approach to take. For hiring labor such as virtual assistants, sites like oDesk.com and Elance.com are great choices, where practically all kinds of labor is available on demand.

3. *Go somewhere cool, hip and exotic.*

As mentioned earlier, traveling and making people aware of your whereabouts is a strong tool to increase your status. When responding to colleagues or employees, you can intrigue them. Try changing your mails from "I'm on vacation," which is extremely boring. Instead tell them, "I apologize for the delay in getting back to you; I just got back from Ibiza, Bali, etc." So don't be shy to go somewhere fabulous, you deserve it as a winner and people expect you to do so.

How to Build Confidence

Looking at the world around you, the people with the biggest egos and highest self-esteem or self-confidence are often the ones that manage to become winners. Confidence is important, and it is crucial for most entrepreneurs that want to become successful. Have you ever met a salesperson with a lack of self-confidence and even though you wanted to buy the product you actually ended up walking away from the purchase decision for that one reason? Well I have experienced it many times in my life, and when the salesperson is not pushing me too hard but rather shows a self-confidence that makes me want the product even though I didn't plan to buy it, I most likely would end up buying it. So confidence is really and truly something that people should work on developing when dreaming about joining the club of winners.

Let's think about the previous part on talents. From that section we quickly concluded that talent is about the way you practice, and the way you gain and interpret knowledge. Confidence is the same way. When you increase your talent, your confidence tends to follow you, since you become self-confident about the subject that you've mastered. Look at every sport star around you on TV: they often seem so confident when they do everything, and this often leads back to training and the talents they have acquired from that part. The important fact about confident people is that they are willing to acknowledge their weaknesses and do not hesitate to share their opinion with confidence about things they are knowledgeable about.

Confident people acknowledge risk, and they are often more persuasive than others to convince people to join a project even though the risk profile is more averse than they normally would invest in.

A few techniques you can apply to yourself:

Do:

- Be honest with yourself about your own capabilities and what you actually know and do not know!

- Raise your talent by practicing issues you are not good at, such as public speaking, etc.

- Embrace new opportunities and try to master them, instead of fearing them!

Do not:

- Hesitate for a second to ask for an external validation if you need one, since not asking can lower your confidence.

- Lose focus on the goal you have set or let others influence your decisions to an extent that it makes you insecure.

- Worry about what others think about you. Always focus on your own, it is okay to fail—the worst that can happen is that you learn from your mistakes!

A Road Map to a Life that Matters!

What matters in life and what many winners tend to do is to follow a path, which most people do not follow. Winners don't chase money like most realtors do in the States. When it comes to getting a real estate license, I know for a fact that in Florida it can be done easily if you are smart—in literally less than 12 hours. So this creates a problem: Miami, for example, has more than 250,000 realtors "all" hunting for the deals that are $500,000 and up. This is a path a winner would never take. It sounds fairly easy to sell a few expensive houses and then not to work for the rest of the year, but the truth is, that only happens to the best networkers. So what is a "Road Map" that really matters, when you act like a winner?

First of all you need to be unique, you need to realize what matters to you, what will make you happy each day, by using winning tools and strategies to create a living from what you love.

There is no direct path in life and the road to achieve the dream of prosperity and wealth is never straightforward. Most people have to change direction, change jobs, and even go bankrupt down the road, when aiming and trying their utmost to achieve their goals. First and foremost, research suggests that people are in charge of their own luck and destiny. Secondly, the world is changing rapidly so decisions about the future made today can be changed rapidly tomorrow. So my point is, there is really no roadmap to join the club of winners and gain riches. But your chances are much higher when you follow a path that you feel good about and ultimately would be proud of. Creating a meaningful life and having a career that makes you feel happy everyday is closer than you think. If you teach yourself discipline, absorb knowledge, and ultimately use technology to help you, your path is more direct than you ever thought it would be!

Networking by Managing Yourself!

Managing yourself is not always easy. People tend to stick to the thought that "the bigger and more important people I have in my network, the better it is for me." This statement is not entirely true, since important people often rely on a few people in their network, and they all create and share values among the members. Often, people tend to believe that their network is more important than anything else and that it is not about who you are, but who you know. I stick to the belief that people who think that it is all about who you know are misguided in networking, and they would fail! The reasons why I say so is that research has shown that the happier you are, the more likely people are to help you and the more likely you are to make connections that are valuable. Depending on other people would often lead to a failure in friendship or a failure in trust among others. Most people do not care about you at the end of the day, if you aren't a winner you would end up getting hurt.

Many people are afraid of networking and do not know the basic rules of doing so. The question you should ask yourself and try to identify is, are you really network impaired?

Here are examples of how people often make mistakes and take on roles in networking:

• *The formalist* is the person who focuses too much on his or her company's hierarchy, and they would often miss out on opportunities that come from informal connections.

* **The overloaded manager** is networking internally so much and has so much contact with colleagues and external bonds that he or she often becomes a bottleneck to progress and ends up burning out.

* **The superficial networker** is the person that is always engaged in all conversations and want to interact with as many people as possible. This person often mistakenly believes that the size of the network is more important than anything else, and that tends to bring in many superficial people that do not bring you or your company any value.

* **The chameleon** is the person that always changes interests, values, and personality to match the audience around them. The person often ends up being disconnected from the group since no one knows what this person really wants.

* **The disconnected expert** is the person who does not want to build new skills. This person would always stick to people who keep the person focused and safe on his or her existing competencies. If the person does not like change they would never seek it, and stick to people who do not like change either.

* **The biased leader** is the person that often relies on advisers, a network and close ties around the person. The person would always network and work with people like him or herself with the same functional background, location, and/or values. This person seeks to

reinforce his or her biases, but should rather focus on learning from outsiders and seek new knowledge for decision making.

These are the common traits of people who make mistakes unintentionally when networking. The superficial networker is often that guy or girl who, when they speak, tend to know everyone and have tried seemingly everything in life. They tend to brag and they are tough to compete with since they always know someone better etc. The only problem with this personality when you finally ask, "Great, you know this person…can you ask him or her to come and help me with this project, etc." is that the person tends to be less connected than they brag about.

Networking is not an art and it is really not as complicated as many people think! Some people tend to make up titles and other fancy sounding illustrations about themselves, and this is often to make themselves seem more important. Winners tend to see this as noise and they often identify these people right away, and nicely ignore them down the road. A winner is someone who knows how to read people and does not make up stories to make people like them. A winner knows that others like them for who they are and their knowledge, and that's what networking is all about, knowing how to be yourself and avoiding the six traits of impaired networkers!

Stretching Your Global Mindset

Stretching your knowledge about globalization is more important than ever, and every winner is more international than ever before. You can start to think about the world by asking yourself some fundamental questions: How well do I know and understand cultures in other parts of the world? Does what I am doing matter for business or society or both? Do I value everybody the same or do I have more sympathy to certain people around me?

Asking yourself fundamental questions is always a great way to build understanding for others and other cultures and finally traveling support the understanding as well.

Part 4

The "Instant MBA"

"Winning is habit. Unfortunately, so is losing."

-Vince Lombardi

Our world has never seen more MBAs being educated annually than now. Generations ago you used to be considered unique and an asset to an organization if you had a bachelor's degree. Today you are expected to have an MBA at entry-level positions in the corporate world, and having two master's degrees or a PhD is what will often make you stand out. So why is education important when you just become one of the regular people in the work force?

First, education can save you from many failures and create basic knowledge about most operational attributes that organizations encounter on a daily basis. Second, it brings your level of knowledge to a required level, which companies often tend to expect. But in an entrepreneurial world with labor on demand available from former Russian countries, India, Philippines, etc., which can be acquired from $7-8 an hour and up for talented programmers, is it really worth to invest in higher education, if you dream about shaping and creating your own future?

I personally would say it all depends: some people need the ballast of the education that they gain, while others just do it to please their parents and maybe create a safety net for themselves. However, there are many free resources and advice available on the internet today that can help entrepreneurs in knowledge creation. This advice is what I categorize as *"the instant MBA"* which includes different methods to learn how to manage a business overnight.

Make Your Product Viral

Everybody has during the past years been talking about making viral advertising for their products in order to create a free word-of-mouth effect for services or products. The initiatives from companies have been many and they have been extremely creative down the road. The problem is that if you rely on one viral campaign to kick in as your sole source of marketing and it fails, you end up failing. So the question arises: why not make the launch of the product viral itself?

Viral products are a relatively new phenomenon, since the internet has enhanced the production of such products. Look at Skype, a perfect example of a viral product that launched with the effect of peer-to-peer promotion. Other tools are social networks and adding a Facebook "share" button, which can enhance awareness highly throughout the social networks. If an influencer in your network likes a product you might end up liking it or at least checking the product out. Adding a share button actually is proven to increase awareness by 400% in the right conditions as a minimum.

Making a product exclusive in the beginning is often a great way to increase the exposure in the press and by word-of-mouth. Google has done this many times in the past when beta launching their products such as Gmail and Google+, and they turned out to receive a great network effect since they made the product at the launch state viral. Facebook was exclusive initially, and the exclusivity was ultimately what made it cool to be a member at first, and then later they were able to roll it out to the masses while staying "cool." So a great piece of advice to always keep in mind when launching a product or a service is to make it viral and let it to get a life of its own with the masses on the internet.

The Viral Product Landscape

Active

Exclusive launch with personal invitation (Facebook in the start)

Special offers: Groupon, Living Social

User generated such as Facebook and Twitter

Embedded offers Signup from forms

Passive

Automated targeting Recomendations from Amazon

Automated notifications such as Foursquare

Specific Individuals
Broad Population

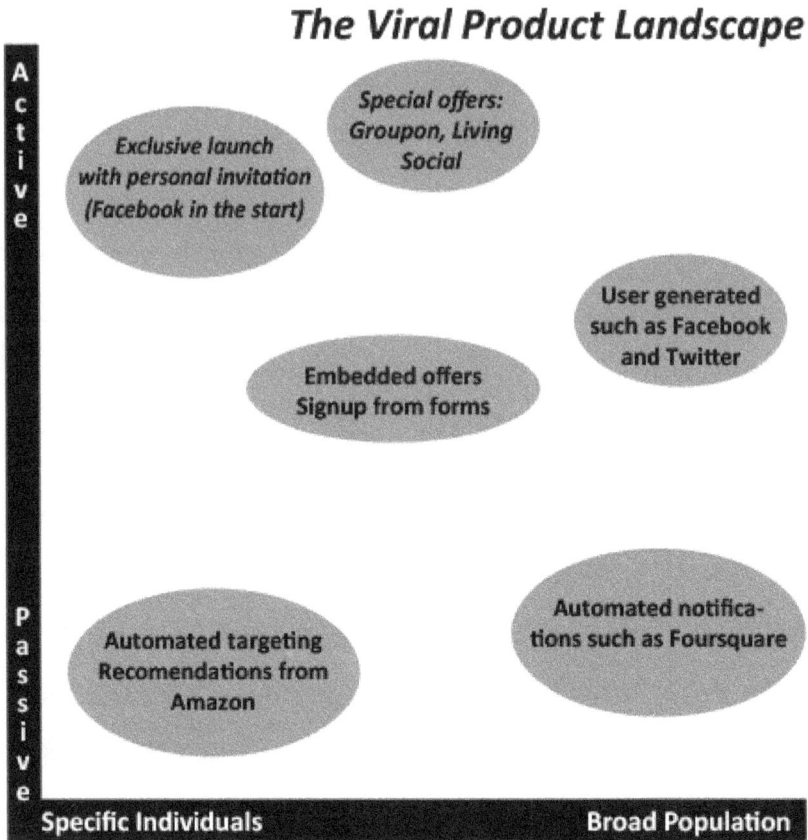

How to Make High-Stakes Decisions

Everyday we make decisions, but once in a while we all run into decisions that can change our lives or careers. Most of us think carefully about the decision but it does require a lot of thoughts and deliberation. When making a decision it is unlikely that a single approach can help you every time you face a high-stakes decision, but some factors are more helpful than others.

First of all, listen to what the knowledgeable people around you know about the decision you have to make. Secondly, most people act differently when there's more at stake. People often tend to take more time when deciding upon something, but at the end of the day it is a magnitude of the outcome that really should determine the time you spend. You should think about what your options are, as well as how the outcome would affect you and the other people involved in the decision. Identify the hazards of the decision and avoid them. When involving people in the process, make sure that you do own the outcome and you would receive the credit needed for making the high-stakes decision. Consulting with others is always smart as long as the decision is not classified. Asking a friend or a colleague for an opinion might be good or bad depending on their risk profile. The only problem when involving others in a decision is when you try to find a consensus, which often makes the decision harder; thus consensus is in most cases not optimal but you should rather act like a leader and make the decisions at the end of the day.

People tend to be close-minded which creates a pitfall, which might close your eyes to the right decision. Being open-minded is never a bad thing and this is truly what separates a winner from the rest. When being open-minded be careful of your own bias, since people tend to have a strong bias against different things. Often you are drawn to have a bias depending on your education, self-interest, or other factors, so acknowledging and knowing your own bias is extremely important. Finally, learn from past experiences, since you can avoid mistakes done in the past. Always reflect and learn what separates a winner from the rest.

A few methods you can apply to your self:

Do:

- Listen to others, but make sure you make the decision on your own at the end of the day.

- Be aware of your own biases and learn how to embrace them in a positive way.

- Feel okay about asking a trusted person for help.

Do not:

- Rely purely on your instinct.

- Think a decision is the same as in the past; the world is changing rapidly and so does the rationale for decisions.

- Ignore new information that can help you make the right decision.

Young People do Embrace Creativity in Organizations

According to the CEO of United Nations Foundation, the biggest mistake in her career was that she didn't bring in enough young people to her organization. She said in an interview with the New York Times, *"If I had it to do over, I'd probably bring more young people into the organization at an earlier stage. I remember Jack Welch of General Electric saying having a young person just out of college as a 'mentor' kept him fresh."* So why are young people good for organizations?

Well first of all, they see the world from a different perspective than the "older" people in the organization do. Secondly, they understand changes and embrace them to an extent. The thing that makes young people important is that they are better at understanding new technologies and interpreting changes for an organization. Look at young startups in Silicon Valley, the new generation of companies being created by incubators all focus on making technology work for people in terms of embracing teamwork and ease of technology. Take a look at Dropbox, an amazing backup tool that two young guys created to ease the sharing of pictures, documents etc. among teams and make a safe method of backing up files—they recently hit a valuation of $5 Billion. Young people embrace technology and observe how people work, and often tend to become creative with solutions to problems most didn't know existed. Being a busy business leader creates problems with the pressure of daily decisions that have to be made, and having a young person on staff near you, to update you, is very important for any business leader or entrepreneur.

You Have to Change with your Customers!

Companies that fail to understand and follow their customers in terms of demand and needs will always fail. Many companies fail in following their customers; the problem is that today the choices are many and if you do not follow them or try to lead them, then you can be sure a competitor will. Winners understand how to react when customers change habits, and they do everything to forecast for their future needs. Look at Dell: they used to be the biggest manufacture of Personal Computers, but they failed to follow the customers' demands, which changed from personalized computers to computers that you physically see in stores and at low prices. Dell thought its strategy was superior and in a short manner of time HP took on and captured that market, since Dell didn't listen and follow its customers. The list of companies that failed to listen could be long, but the important point to learn is the fact that if you do not listen to your customers, your odds of becoming a winner are close to zero percent. Take cellphone carriers, which are all rolling out their "4G" networks since they all believe that their customers want faster service on their smartphones. But there is one thing the carriers were forgetting, which actually led Virgin Mobile to capture a huge part of the market, becoming the fastest company in U.S. history to gross $1 billion in revenue after the initial launch of the company. What Virgin saw was the advantage of becoming a Virtual Mobile Operator (VMO), meaning that they rent time on an established network where that they would offer customer care and lower prices. The carriers are all focused on who has the fastest network while Virgin focuses on giving customers the best price, which ultimately is the right decision. VMOs actually started out of Denmark, where an entrepreneur started the first known VMO service, Telmore. It instantly became a success, and it lowered prices through a price war among the carriers in Denmark, and in the end it benefited the consumers and the VMO. I believe Virgin and Telmore are two great examples of how companies can take on existing markets, change the rules of how business is conducted, actually create a demand, and change what the customer expects.

Use a Rejection As Your Motivator

No product or company is ever perfect, and rejection should be perceived as the best motivator since you have all the chances in the world to get something right the second time. I have seen over and over again in my life people who just chase easy money and get extremely upset from a rejection and move on to the next rejection. What truly sets the winner's personality apart from the rest is that when they encounter a rejection, it is like the best motivation for them. They know that you don't always get it right the first time, and that if you keep trying you will get there one day. The people who just follow money, money, money will often never make the real money. As I see it, it is the ones who understand technology and knowledge and form their company around that. If they're right, the money follows them. Imagine if most people gave up when they receive a rejection, then the world would be widely different and no one would try to create change, since everyone would be afraid to fail. Rejection is not a failure, which most people see it as. I know it sucks to have been working extensive hours on a project and then have people reject you. But the important lesson is that you should not see it as a failure, but rather listen, learn and improve.

If You're Satisfied, You're In Denial – Period!

Often when companies are satisfied, they would encounter a stage of denial and believe they are perfect. As I described about the importance about change and following the customers, this is often an issue that you will encounter when entering that stage toward failure!

Take a look at Myspace, which was way bigger than Facebook at first. Had they known they did something wrong at an early stage and adapted a strategy that would create a strategic fit, Facebook might not have crushed them down the road. The problem is that the management at Myspace was satisfied with the numbers and that it had the biggest social network in the western world at that time. The only problem is that when you encounter this stage, you often ignore potential rivals that could enter the market. Facebook came along and Myspace really first realized the threat after it was too late, becoming like Friendster, a big failure compared to Facebook. Another example is RIM, the manufacture of Blackberry. It had the smartphone market in the U.S. for years, but in a matter of a small time Apple and Google took on RIM and today the company is facing problems, declining market share and huge layoffs. So one issue is really being careful not to become too satisfied with your products or services. Always be critical and ask yourself how you can do something better. This is how companies should think about any product; small changes often equal huge profit or survival for some. A common trait for managers is that when you ask them, what do you think of this product, they would answer something like, "This product is pretty good or amazing." Then you know right away they are in denial; they should say it is good BUT this and that could be improved down the road and that is exactly how a winner thinks.

Your Brand Should Deliver Its Promise, No Matter What

Imagine you walk in to Wal-Mart and after checking the prices you realize they are not the cheapest anymore. This would potentially ruin their brand and people would start going to Target instead, which some customers might have thought of as too expensive before. If you as a brand or company make a promise it is extremely important to deliver on this promise. Look at McDonald's. Why do you think they are so popular, beside the price point? McDonald's delivers consistency: you know you get the same product at any McDonald's around the globe, and you trust their brand. If they started delivering a different burger each time you ordered I am pretty sure most people would seek burgers elsewhere. The problem is that delivering the promise is often what sets apart the winners and the losers. Jeopardizing the brand by failing in terms of delivering a promise is too expensive for any business. Fedex for example would be out of business relatively quickly if they started to deliver too late on most occasions. People are willing to pay a premium to Fedex for the simple fact they believe that they deliver their promise, and they do not trust USPS the same way to do so. So remember to deliver what you would expect of your company as a customer and be consistent!

Take Advantage Of Competitors That Are Easy To Challenge and Tease!

Crushing the weakest competitors is an old strategy but many forget to embrace the busy environment that most face on a daily basis. It is no surprise companies are created to make money and give the owners a return on their investment. Look how HP attacked Dell when Dell started to fail; suddenly it became fairly easy to take on a bigger competitor. Zappos.com realized that most online retailers lacked at service and customer experience so launching a company focusing purely on the experience was something unheard of at first, and this challenges Amazon who later bought Zappos. Oracle and IBM has many examples where one claims something about each other's product and they are always teasing and fighting against each other. The natural fight between competitors is expected, but it is all about realizing the weakness of the other and using it against them in order to gain market share and make more money. So as an entrepreneur aiming to join the club of winners, it is important to identify your rivals and learn all their weaknesses so you can target them and gain customers from their mistakes.

Miss The " Paradigm Shifts," You'll Miss The Future.

Paradigm shifts are something everyone should pay close attention to. If you miss one you would often be out of business. Thomas Kuhn first recognized a paradigm shift in 1962 in his book, *The Structure of Scientific Revolution*. Kuhn identified that a shift in science or technology is not evolutionary but rather is a *"series of peaceful interludes punctuated by intellectually violent revolutions,"* and in those *revolutions "one conceptual world view is replaced by another."*

It does not happen automatically but actually a player who wants to change the market and the rules of the game forces a paradigm shift. An example is the shift in technology that allowed users to shift from regular books to an Amazon Kindle. This shift in the example of Amazon's Kindle has taken many mom-and-pop bookstores out of business, and the paradigm shift is not something they can control or react to, since their businesses are to small. Borders, who recently declared bankruptcy, didn't follow the new paradigm, which was to focus on online business, and close stores to adapt and launch an e-ink reader in time to respond to Amazon and Barnes and Noble.

Motorola missed the paradigm shift from analog to digital phones and Nokia took off like a rocket. Blockbuster didn't see that the model was about to change; consumers' demand changed and Netflix helped the paradigm for the movie rental industry to change. Winning businesses do create paradigm shifts, and those are the businesses that often become worth billions rather than millions. So if you are thinking about starting a business, a paradigm shift is something you can create throughout disrupting an industry and changing the rules of the game.

Legacy is stupid, and you shouldn't care!

Most young entrepreneurs are afraid of failure, especially if their parents were successful in their professional careers. Some people believe they have to take over their parents' company and they are afraid of failing, and when they finally take over the company they either steer it down the drain or make it better. The problem is the people who are afraid of failure often get paranoid about it and end up failing at the end of the day. Look at a winner like Bill Gates: he does not believe in the legacy for his children. As you all know, Bill and his wife Melinda Gates decided to donate most of their money to charity with the clear goal to make the world a better place. Bill does not care about his own legacy: according to him, his children are not going to inherit billions since he does not believe the money would do well for them. He furthermore believes that if people look at his legacy, he does not care what people think, but if he can read 2,000 pages about vaccinations in order to encourage others to do so and fight for making the world a better place, that is all he wishes for. But even though he publicly claims he does not care, his legacy might look better than most billionaires since he is the biggest philanthropist in history. You should never worry about your legacy but rather live on your own and decide what makes you happy and how can you design your life to become a winner!

Part 5

New Business Models:

"The old rules and the old methods of winning are gone."

- Dick Morris

The business landscape is changing rapidly, and the evolution of business models has changed entirely over the years. Back in the 1950s, McDonald's and Toyota were two of the best examples of great business models, which people wrote about and paid attention to. In the 1960s Wal-Mart was seen as an innovator, creating a new low-cost hypermarket that sold everything possible under the same roof. In the 1970s Fedex came to the market and people said that their business model would never work and that they were insane (Guess Fedex's founder Frederick W. Smith is laughing from his yacht today). The 1980s gave us Blockbuster, Home Depot and other specialty stores that became nationwide chains, as well as Apple, Microsoft, Intel, Dell, and other technology companies that dominate today. The 1990s brought us disruption: Southwest in the U.S. and Ryanair in Europe, who both changed the landscape and business models behind airlines to something that was never seen before. So the business models tend to change every 10 years, and with the increase in technology, that change will go faster than ever. This creates a problem for business owners since companies need to respond to market conditions at a much faster rate than ever before. Business models are way more complicated in their design today, since science and research have pushed the limits for what they recommend.

The list of business model design and the way we do business is extremely long today. Alexander Osterwalder, a PhD from Austria, has written perhaps the most comprehensive book about business models, called *Business Model Generation* (2010). Osterwalder created a tool called the "Business Model Canvas," which I recommend everyone to take a look at when looking at his or her existing business or an idea. Besides business models in general the way we interact and work with others has changed rapidly.

Outsourcing became notoriously famous with all the jobs that moved to India in IT and call centers. Crowdsourcing is the newest part of moving tasks outside the company, but crowdsourcing is probably the most comprehensive way to rethink innovation and business development. To explain crowdsourcing in the easiest way I recommend you consider the following:

"A company has a problem that they cannot solve internally and perhaps they didn't succeed with it when they did outsourcing either. So instead of wasting time and money they decide to ask a big group of people to solve the problem. When they come with the solution will the person who solves it receive his money and the company the solution to the problem."

This all sounds very beautiful and easy, letting others do the work—but that is actually the essence of crowdsourcing. The crowdsourcing is estimated to employ around 1 million people worldwide annually and they where paid roughly $1-2 billion last year in earnings. So having a task force that can help on demand sounds easy, and it leaves me with the question: why do other companies not do so today?

The next pages are all written about crowdsourcing and how you can apply it to become a winner in your life!

Crowdsourcing and why does human beings interact and engage in Crowdsourcing?

"Crowdsourcing is supposedly just another easy way to skip R&D cost and gain creative insight? Or is it more complicated than that?"

First, when launching a crowdsourcing project you would need to define your crowd which is the group of people whom you are targeting. Secondly, a call to the crowd needs to be as clear as possible, otherwise they might interpret it differently from the desired solution. The crowd must understand entirely the seekers call (you), since if questions arise for the project scope from the solvers, then you most likely end up failing the project before starting it. **The call to the crowd should not under any circumstances be able to be misunderstood or interpreted in different ways. It has to be clear!** Third, you need to make the rules clear about the payout—if you award more than one winner then how many can win, what contribution is expected from the crowd, how is selection of the winner done, and can the crowd vote for the winner as well?

Finally, you need to create a deadline for the project since a solver might not start the process if he knows that he can't make the deadline, so all basic rules and fairness have to be determined up-front, otherwise the project would most likely fail. Will the contributors receive credit for their work? For some it is better to receive credit than an actual cash reward, How involved are you— will you have time to answer questions from the crowd and provide them with feedback?

All this leads you to an obvious question: why do people engage in crowdsourcing? Is it to be a part of the group, for the money or just recognition?

Looking at the solvers, they are all human beings and according to Maslow (1983), their needs consist of five layers: Physiological, Safety, Social, Esteem and Self-actualization needs. At the first layer we talk basic needs that most of the solvers will have in their everyday life, so if they have food, basic money, etc. why do they engage in crowdsourcing?

One could say that they engage to make more money to be able to take more vacations, buy more things in their everyday needs. People are different and the studies suggest that there are three scenarios for interaction between human beings, according to Maslow.

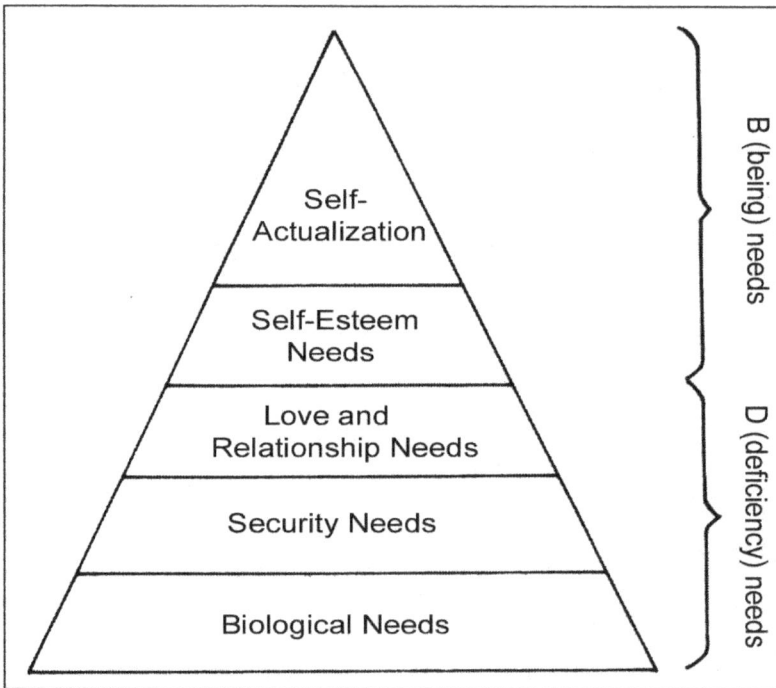

Maslow in Crowdsourcing:

1.   Humans build needs upon needs and always want more, so some solvers will engage in crowdsourcing solely for the money.

This can both be good or bad in the sense that their work is rewarded at the end. These personalities will never become the brand ambassador for the company they solved for if they know the seeker. They will just perform a task and receive the reward. A winner would be careful about how to engage these types of users for some tasks.

2.   Human needs at the fourth level are Esteem needs, which are recognition, self-esteem and status for their participation. This is great for companies or entrepreneurs since these personalities have traits that lead to bragging and telling others about their work! Payment is not the sole award for these personalities, who serve as great ambassadors for your product and brand.

3.   Humans like social needs, and when they engage in a crowd they get the sense of a social belonging in a project, which satisfies the third level. The fourth level is satisfied because you will receive a reward, recognition that gives you a status among your peers and finally stimulates your self-esteem. When receiving a cash award the person would be able to fill out the gaps in their hierarchy of needs and this is the ultimate solution for many seekers to acquire this solver personality.

In all three cases the solvers have traits that are similar but yet different. As described, an interaction between number two and three creates a perfect fit for most seekers, since the solver is involved beyond an economic reasoning.

Can a regular consumer become a solver and an idea creator in companies and does interaction between customers and organizations work in reality?

It does, and the reasoning for the consumers to interact is often the second level of behavior; they are either angry with the company through a bad experience or they simply just love the brand or company and want to engage in enhancing the products and future development. Dell, Starbucks, and many other consumer brands have seen the trend through their own website to create forums to interact and receive ideas. This has been working fine the past years but social media such as Facebook and Twitter are changing the landscape with direct consumer interaction in product development. Customer Relation Management (CRM) tools such as Salesforce's solution comes with crowdsourcing add-ons for the organization to track and gain ideas from its customers. Today the social landscape is changing rapidly and even in industries that did not listen to the consumer in the past, companies now more than ever focus on customer care through social channels.

The 4 Types of Crowdsourcing

Crowdfunding

In the recent year, crowdfunding has become more relevant than ever. Several online businesses practice this principal as their business model. Crowdfunding is fundamentally the collective cooperation, trust, and attention from people who fund and sometimes donate money to great ideas. Kickstarter.com is a great example where people post a project they want to do, along with the incentives to help fund it. If the project receives the minimum they ask for, their funding is in place and they relatively quickly raised money for interesting projects that other normally wouldn't fund for them.

Crowdfunding is historically best known and mostly used for a disaster that appears, like the earthquakes in Haiti and Japan, where significant capital was raised in as short a time as possible. People collect money into a big pool to support an effort toward helping a cause. Crowdfunding can be separated into two manners of use: for non-profit organizations and for profit ideas, creative work such as art, movies and simple efforts to start up funding for a business. A good example of a crowdfunding campaign on a large scale is Obama's campaign for office in 2008. He managed to crowdfund $137 million online in only 24 hours. This extravagantly high number proves that Obama succeeded with crowdfunding, and he was the first presidential candidate in the states to use social media and crowdfunding for a campaign contribution method. This campaign showed the power behind crowds and gathering them together—small or large funding amounts do not matter as long as the crowd is enormous. That's what truly mattered in Obama's case, and they succeeded.

Crowdfunding can also be used to help developing countries to support entrepreneurs by investing money in people with an idea that normally would have no other way to gather money. Sites like Kiva.com and the Danish startup MyC4.com utilize crowdfunded microloans to these people and they would if possible pay back down the road with an interest rate. Sites like this take crowdfunding into a broad social and philanthropic tool with incentives to make money for all. Other examples are crowdfunded microloans to normal Americans and Europeans, to fund education, car loans, etc., that would be denied in the local bank. These types of loans are in essence crowdfunding but some people refer to them as "peer to peer" loans as well. Prosper.com was the first to revolutionize that market, and it again proved the fundamental belief in the crowdfunding strategy to work.

Crowdfunding is also becoming a new phenomenon at the venture capital / seed stages. Since most people wish to join the club of winners, companies like GrowVC (Grow Venture Community) are worth paying attention too. They are the latest example of an innovative business model addressing the needs in the field for venture capital and funding of startups. How GrowVC works is that the members choose together online which startups to fund, and they then provide their advice to the companies as mentors, together as a crowd. This is for some not very ideal from both sides, since you as a business owner suddenly have 100+ investors and not only when big to deal with and listen too. If the crowd picks something you don't want to invest in, you might end up unhappy. However, at the end of the day the overall belief of the crowdfunding platform is extremely successful on the non-profit funding site, and on funding for startups and microloans we are moving toward a working trend that would raise over time.

Crowd-creation / Crowd-Casting

Crowd-creation is the most common way of doing a crowdsourcing methodology. Crowd-creation is in its basics, how one crowd solves a specific task. Crowd-creation exists in many variations from the creation of the Operating System Linux, the way Innocentive (a site helping solvers and seekers to meet) and Threadless.com (T-shirt store using crowdsourcing) operate, to mention a few. When you use a crowd to help your company, this creates many different variations and possible solutions of a problem, and as most people know, many heads think better than one. Basically said, a crowd-creation is when a seeker submits a problem to solvers and they create a solution for the seeker.

Crowd-casting is on the other hand the principle of building a network of customers/users and initiating tasks or challenges to be solved with the sole purpose of creating innovative products or market insight. Proctor and Gamble actually created their product Swiffer through crowd-creation on Innocentive.com.

Crowd-casting is known at business schools around the globe, where companies create competitions for students to solve a business case. This is done at Copenhagen Business School annually, where they run their case competition. By doing so the companies do two important things: connect with future possible employees or customers and secondly gain insight and ideas from students. The case competition at Copenhagen Business School is a perfect example of crowd-casting in essence and practice. This means that winners and winning companies are often the ones that are better at involving the crowd since they are open and don't mind receiving new inputs and ideas to grow.

Crowd-voting

Crowd-voting is the function of letting the crowd decide what a company should produce by votes and ranking. Crowd-voting is the allocation of funds or time for the given project or cause. Often, consumer brands like Dell or Starbucks use this method to utilize the ranking from all the ideas the customer generates. When the consumers vote and comment on each set of the ideas, it is often the most demanded that shows up with most votes, and the company has an easier time finding the most important cause to start working on in order to innovate or improve customer service and satisfaction. Another version of crowd-voting in general is reality TV-shows as seen all over the world with Idols and X–Factor. The crowd actually ends up choosing the winner by texting in the end or at least has one of the biggest decision factors in real time for the outcome of the show. Threadless, as previously mentioned, is based on crowd-voting to utilize the crowd-creations in order to estimate demand and forecast what the crowd wants, since they actually tell Threadless.com what to produce and how many T-shirts they can expect to sell. For Threadless, this is truly unique since they "always" produce what need and do not end up with a big stock of shirts.

Crowd-Wisdom

Crowd-wisdom is the methodology of using a crowd's wisdom together to solve a problem. The crowd will often have a broader knowledge about a subject combined than any individuals. Jeff Howe, the author of *Crowdsourcing*, states that:

"Given the right set of conditions the crowd will almost always outperform any number of employees – a fact that many companies are increasingly attempting to exploit."

The newest matters in crowd-wisdom are Twitter—recent research shows that Twitter is the best way to predict the stock market today, when using sites like Stocktwits.com. I do not believe that many if any stockbrokers actually study streams on Twitter about companies they invest in or the market itself. New research claims that Twitter predicts the stock market 87.6% of the time, so by that simple proof the crowd has more power than people think, according to Businessinsider.com. So if new channels like these are more efficient, one could ask oneself: why does everyone not use such channels? The answer is obvious...most people are afraid of the unknown, and often winners are the ones that would experiment and find new ways to do things.

Disadvantages and Dangers When Doing Crowdsourcing

If you consider crowdsourcing, there are obvious and not-so-obvious potential disadvantages to consider for any organization or entrepreneur. Most of them are not obvious, since people tend to focus on the benefits when choosing an uncertain method of business development strategy. Cognitive restructuring is when a person thinking about a certain issue one way, and they change their vision towards more accuracy down the road. This is often a danger for businesses since they might see the trees grow into the sky without realizing downsides with the strategy chosen when they do not open their minds. Crowdsourcing will always bring in an uncertainty to any project and whether the crowd will perform as predicted, or whether we end up with an outcome that kills the project, are possibilities to consider.

• **1**. Confidentiality is the first part of possible considerations for any crowdsourcing project. This is since there is a substantial uncertainty combined with the risk. One question could arise, will our competitor have an account that follows all crowdsourcing initiatives in the industry and therefore be able to get the same idea when launching to the crowd, even on sites like Innocentive? The dangers are different when talking about crowd-voting: the company becomes more public, since customers or solvers will vote on something known. Crowd-voting will often be visible to the competitors and they could as well benefit from the crowd's advice towards the company that runs a crowd-voting concept and this is the free flow of information that becomes a danger. Crowd-wisdom is less dangerous than other methods, since you often ask for a Non Disclosure agreement (NDA) and remain anonymous from the crowd and competitors through companies such as Innocentive.com. When companies are choosing crowdsourcing, confidentiality is a part that should be considered when choosing the method of crowd gathering.

◆ **2.** Poor quality and entries irrelevant for the company and the project are often time consuming, and this can become a towering hurdle for the person conducting and reviewing the results and ideas. Companies gathering wisdom on Facebook and Twitter often hit that wall, where too much nonsense and under qualified results can come in as noise. This is an obvious problem and also why when this occurs, crowd-voting automatically filters the brightest ideas to the top and the nonsense in the bottom—but that being said, a lot of resources could be relocated to filter and monitor. These are all aspects that an organization should consider.

◆ **3**. Wrong directions can often be the outcome of ideas if the solvers do not understand the idea or problem to begin with. This is a two-sided problem that consists of creating a clear task for solvers and to understand how solvers must and would understand and read the task. Be clear and specific to avoid direction problems, which could be a waste of time as well, if not done right.

◆ **4**. Popularity misleads is when a company conducts a crowd-voting methodology and this often will happen if the customers vote on a casted idea that has nothing to do with the product area or ideas the company wishes to perform. So again, filtering ideas before votes appear on something that might be very useless is important.

◆ **5**. Stolen or recycled names often occur among solvers or contestants in crowdsourcing competitions. It has sometimes been shown that in design competitions, companies end up receiving a logo that they approve that actually is an exact copy of someone else's, even though they have no way of knowing this. This could potentially end up resulting in a lawsuit for the company as well as huge cost to change the logo, brand, and strategy in the market positioning, and this could harm the company's image and financially take a company out of business.

◆ **6**. Derailment is not acceptable when it is used the wrong way. A notable example is when NASA wanted to crowdsource the name for a room to the International Space Station (ISS). The American comedian Stephen Colbert found it amusing to suggest people vote for his name on TV, and Colbert actually ended up having over 40 thousand votes more than the second most popular option. This was clearly not NASA's intention at the start with, which shows crowds can sometimes derail your project.

◆ **7**. Coming up empty is one of the dangers of engaging in crowdsourcing. Companies can receive suggestions that do not solve the problem or create insight as hoped for, instead resulting in ideas that are not suitable for the company. So it's not guaranteed that you as a seeker end up getting what you hope for, and you could end up empty-handed which is a loss of time and money.

◆ **8**. Missing the best talent! – It is not guaranteed that the best talent to come up with your solution is participating in the crowdsourcing project engaged by the seeker. Some of the best talents can be focused on a very few tasks, and crowdsourcing sometimes might just address and target the people out of work trying to make extra money. It can also be professionals devoting time on both their day job and solver activities in crowd networks. However, most likely the crowdsourcing brings a mass but particularly not the best talent in one field directly, which can be both beneficial and unsatisfactory.

◆ **9**. Hidden costs can be many when considering crowdsourcing as a way of doing New Product Development. Looking through all the ideas, suggestions, and submissions that companies receive can occupy some full-time employees, which can be fine in many cases. But when companies are targeting specific ideas or suggestions they will need professional or legal help to evaluate these since there can come legal risks such as an infringement with intellectual property, and these types of expenses can skyrocket in some instances. That being said most larger new product development, especially in the U.S.—would need legal expertise at the end of the day, so depending on industry, situation, etc. there are downsides in terms of cost in any new product development.

Crowdsourcing Strategies

When you as an entrepreneur or employee in a company are considering doing a crowdsourcing strategy there are some great principles I suggest that you follow. Since every process when thinking about product or business development tends to be a fun, interesting, and chaotic journey, it is the strategy that is extremely important and what often separate winners from the rest.

Crowdsourcing is all about change, in one sense. Companies are turning more and more to external knowledge, with various forms of knowledge sources, this is often to solve more complex tasks.

According to Henry Chesbrough (2003) who was one of the first to do a lot of research about "open innovation," a company that faces complex tasks can rely on their internal knowledge, known as *"closed innovation,"* and the external knowledge, which is known as *"open innovation."* In the traditional system, companies would engage with lead users when opening up to their external sources, according to MIT professor Eric Von Hippel (2005) and learn from them in order to solve or improve ideas/products. Companies might often not think about engaging in crowdsourcing strategies, when opening up to external environments, but just stay intact with a few customers and lead users. This is a hurdle for many companies, since they do not reach out to non-existing customers and figure out how to capture those as well. In addition, the underutilizing of the crowd is a disadvantage that many companies do not understand that, they can gain knowledge, cut cost, etc. by engaging with a crowd in order to sustain and grow their business. Research done by Schrage (2003) shows that when organizations do innovation they must do improvisation, which means you *"do not follow the rules of the game"* like others do. Changing the rules of the game and the industry might create a paradigm shift for businesses and actually aim to create either a Blue Ocean strategy or a simple game-changer.

If companies manage to change the rules rigorously and revise them down the road, their changes for success, according to Schrage (2003), are much higher. Blue Ocean strategies could in cases be linked to crowdsourcing strategies. Often companies by mistake, or by listening to their customers or the *"crowd"* around them, end up creating a game-changer or actually a new market within the market. Take the iPhone as an example. Apple did not think about creating the App Store in public first, but it was the hacking community that actually created their own App Store, which Apple later adapted to. In their case, the crowd and customers showed Apple a need, which they might not have discovered on their own. Apple did introduce the App Store, which in June 2011 has sold more than 15 billion Apps and is one of the highest generators of revenue for Apple today. How did Apple do it? They simply listened to their core users and the crowd. The App store changed the mobile industry, and Apple did create a Blue Ocean within the industry that no one saw coming, maybe not even Apple. The problem is that when companies fulfill a need and listen to customers, and then create blockbusters like Apple and others did, the competition becomes bullish and very quickly they would react in a defensive way and copy you. In many cases product development like iOS and Android in the cell phone industry is pushing the barriers for the physical limits of the products, and this pushes the hardware producers to create a shift for them, where they need to improve the products radically, and the whole crowdsourcing cycle leads to overall improvements.

According to Chesbrough (2003), *"Companies that don't innovate, die."* This statement is spot-on, and if Apple didn't adapt the App Store, Android most likely would have taken the opportunity and Apple might not have been in the position they are today. Look at Research in Motion and Nokia; both failed to innovate, and they both see huge decline in their market share and stock value as a result. The examples of such situations are many, and the list can go on.

The fact is that the Internet over the past 10 years has created platforms, communication, and collaboration that companies were not used to, and this all combined to support creation and adaption of crowdsourcing. According to a research done by Malone et al. (2009) the internet is one of the reasons why companies have to innovate differently through new channels today. He acknowledges the verge of the internet in his research. Lego is a great example of a company that built a product through open innovation, called Lego Mindstorms. They created it with help from MIT Sloan, the software and sensors to the product.

Lego launched the product and quickly after the launch customers started to hack the product and create a different version and programming features. Lego actually went out and got help from the crowd of "*hackers*" that modified the product instead of suing them. This led Lego to connect to a big group of lead users as well as improving the products without extensive R&D costs.

Utilizing the Internet, as a part of a strategy for companies is important, if it is in closed forums online or in the public eye, social media – the presence and speed of change is crucial in most industries, and especially in tech related businesses.

Companies globally are adapting more and more to crowdsourcing initiatives, and the fact that a company can hire thousands of creative individuals that have to come up with a new logo design and other visual wishes gives them an advantage. This is outstanding since you might end up receiving an identity and creativity that is more in harmony with the message that you originally expected. Secondly, instead of paying one ad agency for the task and relying completely on their expertise, you end up getting a deeper horizon for less. Amazon.com and Doritos Chips from Canada are among the brands that have crowdsourced their designs on Crowdspring.com. This shows that larger corporations are moving from pure R&D into crowdsourcing but also use it as a tool for creativity now, which is helping them to save money and enhance their performance. The world has changed over the past many years and "Moore's law" about change is progressing rapidly, which ultimately is what some tech companies is experiencing on a daily basis. Therefore, crowdsourcing is just one of the tools to make a difference, and it is certainly a buzzword of tomorrow.

Crowdsourcing tools

Crowdsourcing is, as described earlier, an open call to a crowd, and this call needs to be handled through some type of system or tool. Tools and the differentiation between the offerings all depend on the desired methodology the company wishes to follow. Creators—in this case the solvers—need a platform in the form of a virtual space to engage in activities. Members of a crowdsourcing mechanism do require some kind of location to engage in activities, which is in most cases a virtual space. These types of platforms need to support team building of some sort, since tasks in crowdsourcing require teams in many cases, along with participation among the peers.

Often it is the case that companies need to define what type of crowdsourcing they are utilizing, as described throughout the analysis, and what benefits there are when selecting a platform designed for the purpose. It is necessary to define the profile of a desired participant to attract that profile through the right channel and platform. Today many platforms exist from the different areas of crowdsourcing:

Crowdfunding :

Kiva.com, Prosper.com, GrowVC.com

Crowd-creation / Crowd-casting:

Innocentive.com, Innobright.com

Crowd-voting:

DELL Ideastorm, Starbuck my idea, Crocs shoes plus many others

Crowd-wisdom

Stocktwits.com, Twitter.com, Facebook.com and other social media entities

"*In the end of the day Crowdsourcing is one of the tools that winners would prefer to use, due to the vast of information and in reality it is the cheapest way to gain creativity. Think about the possibilities with crowdsourcing and beware about the addressed dangers and pitfalls it might bring.*"

– Jesper Qvist

Beware of cheap labor, you get what you pay for

Outsourcing a job is another common way winners obtain cheap labor and get things done. The only problem is that in most cases when finding talent on oDesk.com, Elance.com, etc., you might end up with a very slow person that promises to deliver in three weeks, when in reality it takes them 3-4 months and they start to ask for more money, and have around 1000 excuses. This is the problem when you hire labor that you do not pay enough for, in my experience. I have on several occasions worked with cheap labor, and the issues are always the same, so if you end up with the ones charging a bit more you get what you expect. Imagine the ones that charge less do it for two reasons:

They already work and want to make some extra pocket money after work, and this eventually slows down the speed since many things happen in a project period.

They don't have a job since they are not talented enough and do not have what it takes to deliver the solution you expect, and this delays it ultimately.

My recommendation is to be aware when hiring labor on contract to do your website, program, design, etc. My experience is that you get more for your dollars in the Philippines over India, for example, and they do work more for the money. I might be biased, but Google the issues and many others agree upon this issue. At the end of the day when choosing the right people, motivate them and give them awards for delivering more at an earlier stage, and be careful paying too much upfront.

Case Study 1 about Crowdsourcing - Threadless.com: The Customers are the company!

The story on how Threadless.com was created according to the founders, happened to be an *"accidental business"*. How they without knowing redefined user driven innovation to a new according to them "hyped" term called crowdsourcing. Threadless.com is today one of the most well known examples of companies that have pioneered online business into crowdsourcing and still are growing and highly profitable.

Threadless were started by two high-school dropouts, having no idea about who Von Hippel was and his definition of user driven innovation. They started Threadless.com as a grassroots design community for T-Shirts. People would design and vote on the T-Shirt they liked and they produced and sold them for 15 USD, which in average lead to a 30% profit margin. In the first years,

Threadless.com did not spend any money on marketing and neither did they hire any designers, advertising agencies etc. to help them. But somehow Threadless.com quickly became a success with as many as 100.000 people design, buying and voting on a daily basis. According to Nickell one of the founders they never produced a *"flop"* a t-shirt that did not sell, since they only produced the T-Shirt that people actually demanded (*winning* strategy). According to a Harvard professor in the start it was hard to classify what they did so different. The question clearly was, were it user driven innovation, crowdsourcing or open innovation that made them different? *"Threadless completely blurs that line of who is a producer and who is a consumer, the customers end up playing a critical role across all its operations: idea generation, marketing, sales forecasting. All that has been distributed."* (Karim Lakhani, Harvard Business School). This model where back in the early 2000's very new and first in 2010 beginning to be adapted. According to the two founders the growth and the first two years of operation was just fun for Jake Nickel and Jeffrey Kalmikoff. In 2002, they decided to go full time with Threadless and created it to a profitable business. Later they introduced a price award for a chosen design on $150 to the designer, plus they would receive a free T-shirt with their design. One artist Gleen Jones states in an interview that the price did not matter it was the pride to see my design on the t-shirt and people buying it. Later they increased the cash prices to $500-$2.500. This attracted even more designers, and expanded the thinking of crowdsourcing since it now has become a business on both sides. The whole interaction on Threadless were rather unique for their time, and today 10 years later even global companies like DELL and Havaianas (a Brazilian flip-flop maker) launched design competition on Threadless.com a t-shirt store to award designs on special laptops and the Brazilian Flip-Flop brand which is the most widely used flip-flop in the U.S.

Besides the coolness of adding designs on a laptop and flip-flops, offers from other indirect competitors arrived over time. Urban Outfitters contacted co-founder and CEO Jake Nickell back in 2005 and wanted to sell Threadless shirts in their 150 retail stores throughout United States. The giant retailer Target which is the second largest retailer in the us after Wal-Mart did the same, but Nickell believed that this could make his brand un-cool and they would lose their customer base. Threadless is basically, a company for its customers run by its customers. The growth has been steady as shown:

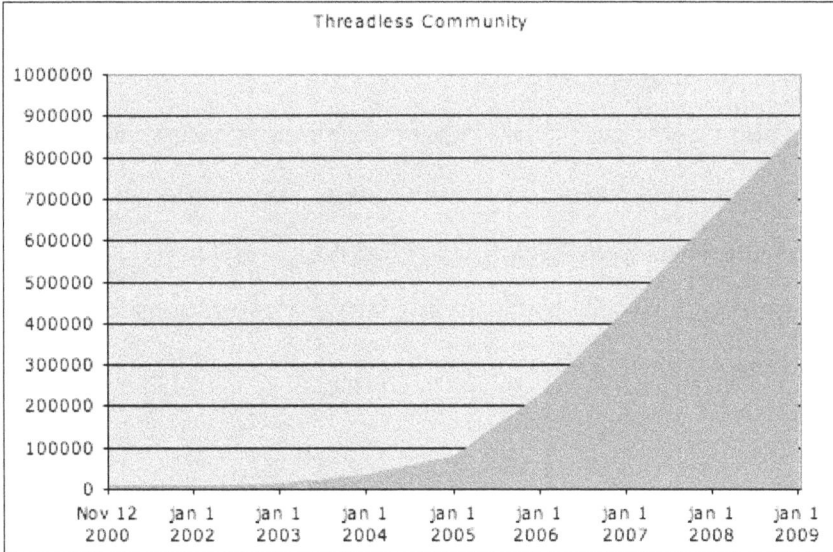

Threadless Community

Imagine Threadless where run by a regular Entrepreneur with a vision to sell t-shirts online! Back in 2000, a few companies survived the burst of the first bubble and managed to growth. In 2006 Threadless.com managed to create $18 million in revenues and growth to $30 million in 2007 (Insight Venture Partners). For a website only selling T-Shirts, generated by the users and selling around $15 to $18, this leads to a total sale for around 2 million t-shirts in 2007. Today Eric Von Hippel redefines the concept behind Threadless and he states that *"Threadless has tapped into a fundamental economic shift, a movement away from passive consumerism Eventually, Threadless-like communities could form around industries as diverse as semiconductors, auto parts, and toys. "Threadless is one of the first firms to systematically mine a community for designs, but everything is moving in this direction,".*

Eric Von Hippel: *"foresees research labs and product-design divisions at manufacturing companies being outstripped by an "innovation commons" made up of tinkerers, hackers, and other devout customers freely sharing their ideas. The companies that win will be the ones that listen."* These scenarios are more and more being adapted globally today, in any larger organizations from Dell, Nike, Lego to Starbucks.

Case Study 2 about Crowdsourcing - Innocentive: The crowd solves your problems!

Innocentive is an excellent example of the classical way of thinking about crowdsourcing. Innocentive connects problem solvers and companies together all under a non-disclosure agreements. Innocentive claims to be the leader in Open Innovation and they claim to be number one in problem solving that cannot be done internally in most organizations. Innocentive's name origins from the two acronyms *innovation* + *incentive* = Innocentive and they connect problem solvers and companies from around the globe. Projects on Innocentive vary in prices from a few thousand dollars to up to 1 million dollars depending on the scope. The problem solvers (the individuals in the crowd) will try to solve the task and if the company picks the winner, the solver will sign any patents and rights over to Innocentive who then signs it to the company so they never meet or know each other. Innocentive are different from other crowdsourcing sites since they will analyze the best solutions for the seeker (company) so they do not have to look through all solution if they are extremely busy. Innocentive then charges a percentage fee of the job for providing the contact, advices and platform. This seems remarkably straightforward and in fact, it is, but most companies yet have not thought out of the box and done so.

Innocentive does not only provide diversity in their portfolio of collaborators but also provides access to these collaborators that companies normally would not be able to accept or access. Proctor and Gamble one of the worlds biggest consumer brands, are one of the frequent clients of Innocentive, when they back in 2000 started a competition on Innocentive to solve a problem they could not handle internally, they did not realize upfront the potential. P&G received many solution ideas and actually ended up with a new product category which where a big driver in their revenues and new market sales hereafter. The product that where invented was Swiffer. Swiffer were not thought about internally but it came out from two problem solvers a high school student from the US and a retired engineer from Austria that combined had this solution for P&G (Innocentive case study, 2009). The reason why P&G is gaining success from Innocentive is the fact that engineers often are "locked" into one topic or idea, and they actually focus within this research topic, which gives them a tough time looking out of the box. Innocentive offers open minds that might know a lot about the topic but actually not locked-in to it on a daily basis and therefore can see it differently. Innocentive have to collaborate with Social Medias and they use sources such as Facebook, Twitter and other Social Medias to attract seekers and solvers into Innocentive. Innocentive as a company in average charge 20% fee for the transaction and a membership fee for the seekers to maintain a certain quality and security for their solvers. But overall they provider a winners solution, and they provide you with a great tool for *innovation*.

Part 6

What does it take?

"I am prepared to try everything once!"

Richard Branson, Founder – Virgin Group

So the obvious question is, what does it take to become a winner and why are some people continuously more successful than others?

As the illustration shows, winners talk ideas and they constantly think about how they can create value for themselves and others, or how they can improve a concept.

Thinking about the issues and business models addressed in the book is a part of the answer of how to become a winner and why some people are brilliant at what they do. Hard work is not always the answer to your prayers. If you know how to adapt strategies such as crowdsourcing, finding the right talents, outsourcing to the right people, and identifying business models that will create a paradigm shift and disrupt a market, you are on the right track. These are some of the main factors that winners tend to be good at. The problem is that only a few people can create all these types of unique businesses, and only a few succeed. But there are other ways to create a winning lifestyle. Look at the ecosystem in Silicon Valley; bubble or not, they keep adding new multi-million dollar contracts to new startups, some of which might make you think, why didn't I do that!?!?

Often creating new inventions is all about your knowledge, hard work, and creativity. The great thing is if you are not the most creative person you can learn from others, crowdsource your creativity, learn the game, raise venture capital, and hire others to do the work, while you seem like the important founder of a great startup. Rethinking your ways to raise money and create awareness is what this part is all about!

Raising Money

Raising money is extremely important for a startup, since most people cannot afford to work on their idea with a limited income—or none—for a longer period. Winners often know that raising money is not only giving away equity of your startup to someone else, but if you happen to give equity to the right person, it can be worth more than the equity received. Winners know that networking and the network of their investors is initially what separated them from becoming the next big thing, when they have the potential. An accomplished entrepreneur friend of mine once told me: *"It is better to own a smaller piece of a huge pie, than owning a large piece of a tiny, tiny pie."* These really are words that all entrepreneurs should remember, since you should involve some people in a project that initially gives you value that you would never have been able to receive on your own. For new startups the ecosystem around raising capital is often very systematic, which means that first you are expected to borrow or raise funds from friends and family. After that you will be able to raise from an angel investor, which I believe is the most important step of any entrepreneur's life. An angel investor is often a person with money who in the past created a great company and now wants to help others become successful and in return make some good money. Incubators are among that circle of importance of angel investing, and a spree of them have been opening the past years.

Y-Combinator

Paul Graham founded Y-Combinator in 2005, and it is known as the "Harvard" of incubators. They invest only $17,000 for one founder and $20,000 in companies with two or more founders. The program has a three-month incubating period and Y-Combinator doesn't provide that much money, while they take 6% of the company in return. The idea is not that these companies are getting loaded with money, but they rather are learning and developing the business with Y-Combinator to a much higher level. Y-Combinator has a demo day for all the "graduating" companies that went through the system and all the venture capital companies are usually there to spot the next big thing, and they are not shy to show the dollars on the spot. The main idea for Y-Combinator is really to incubate these babies, so down the road their money would come back 10- or 20-fold. Among the companies that came from their "eco-system" are two-billion-dollar valuated companies

AirBnB.com (the leading rental place for rooms while traveling) and Dropbox.com (the backup system you had no idea you could live without). Recently on the venture capital scene a guy named Yuri Milner showed up with incredible investments, and he decided with famous venture capitalist Ron Conway to offer all Y-Graduates $150,000 in exchange for a percentage of ownership. Offers like these really show that if you make it to Y-Combinator you are sure to become a winner, at least for a while. Y-Combinator has overall invested about $5 million in companies that they have incubated but, they are estimated to be worth more than $4.7 billion!

Techstars

Techstars is another big incubator in the startup scene of technology companies that are around. Techstars has four locations(Boston, Boulder, Seattle, and New York City), which is different than the other well-known incubators. Techstars focuses on companies outside the *"Valley"* and provides up to $18,000 ($6,000 per founder, allowing up to three) in exchange for 6% of equity in the company, and like Y-Combinator they deliver mentorship, advice and after the three months easier access to venture capital with their demo days. Techstars has gone global and can be found in 20 different countries today, so the odds that you can get into Techstars and receive funding are higher than with Y-Combinator. Techstars has as of 2011 a success rate of 75%, where their graduates actually receive additional funding for growth, which also means the founders ultimately get closer to becoming winners.

Venture Capital

Venture capital is something that most entrepreneurs want to raise if possible for many reasons. Venture capital is the next stage after incubators like Techstars and Y-Combinator. When you have graduated from three months of incubation or get a great angel investor, your odds to close a venture capital deal is much higher and rewarding. This is for many reasons. Number one is to get a high valuation of your startup or company that gives you a real evaluation that you can use to raise even more capital in the bank. Raising money is also often the driver to magnificent growth. Sequoia, Greylock, Founders Fund, Digital Sky Technologies, SV Angel, Kleiner Perkins, and Benchmark are among the vast pool of leading venture capital firms, which means if you manage to raise money from any of them it is considered a big approval of your talent and company. Raising venture capital is not easy and if you do not have a great incubator or angel investor to advise and help you there are a few rules winners should be aware of.

The Elevator Pitch

Venture capitalists (VCs) get spammed with ideas and people who want them to invest in their ideas, which they believe is the next big thing. The problem is you need to practice how to be short and explain your business in a few words. The elevator pitch is a famous concept for an entrepreneur since they should be able to explain their business in less than 30 seconds so that people understand it. Consider it as a **"High-Concept-Pitch"** and prepare yourself. The **"High-Concept-Pitch"** could be written down to a few keywords. Let's take one of my businesses, Voogy (voogy.com). The tagline is *"Like oDesk or Ebay for print,"* depending on who you approach. The thing is when you approach a venture capitalist you need to create a ten-slide **"deck"** that explains your business very quickly for the VC. The deck is a PowerPoint presentation explaining a problem, solution, marketing, concept, and financials.

Forget getting them to sign a Non Disclosure Agreement (NDA), since first they will never do so, and second they receive so many inquiries that advising one and investing in another would be impossible if they sign an NDA, so forget about it!

Traction

You need to create traction in order to attract a VC. As I've described, the best way is often to go through an incubator since they would develop and help you create market traction, which is a part of proving your concept. Without traction it would be rare that they would invest in you, but then again if you are a winner with a track record you might get the money before the company is born. But at the end of the day the VC is looking for the traction that you would create for your product/company, and if it is there your odds to raise capital and get the meeting are way higher and do not equal zero percent!

Get introduced to a VC

Introduction to a VC is the easiest way to get the meeting, and if you do not have the biggest traction and press coverage yet, this is most likely your only way to get that meeting with the VC. Like anyone else, VCs do not like to waste their time, and when they receive hundreds of inquiries for a meeting daily, the one from a friend or an acquaintance would often be the one that gets the meeting. So you could ask yourself the obvious question: who makes the best introduction for me?

1. The incubator / angel Investor (established networks and want their investment to grow)

2. Your advisory board (one of the reasons to bring them on board as well)

3. Your lawyer or accountant might know a great VC

4. Your network in general (if you don't have one, you should start)

Your next step is to send your elevator pitch (ten-slide deck) to your friend or acquaintance so they can pass it on to a VC in their network. This is the best way to get an introduction, since the VC reviews the "**deck**" and quickly decides to do the meeting or not.

The Perfect Deck

Since down the road you would need to raise capital if you want to do big business and become a winner, the deck is extremely important as a sales tool to investors. An example of a perfect "**deck**" is illustrated in order below:

1. **Cover** – You need to include your logo and tagline (like "Company X is like Facebook for business," something they can relate to).

2. **Summary** – The concept, where you use your *"elevator pitch,"* since this is the best way to summarize it all.

3. **Team and Advisory Board** – Any VC would like to know if the people who they invest in would be able to deliver the job and the people are often of main importance in many cases.

4. **Problem** – Explain the problem. With Voogy, we identified that when companies order print jobs, it is very hard to find the best price since there is no market place, and ordering is not easy – so that's a real-life business situation that has a problem.

5. **Solution** – Well obviously we see Voogy as the solution to the problem, we simply created a market solving the problem described above.

6. **Marketing** – How would you market the product? Do not just count on a TechCrunch press release, then forget about raising the money you need!

7. **Technology** – Today, technology is important but also easier and cheaper to develop, so show the VC the proof of concept and how your technology makes a difference.

8. **Competition** – Who are your competitors and what are their weaknesses that you have identified? Don't deny competition, since every industry has it; fighting against others is always an interesting case and could be very giving in terms of $$$.

9. **Sales, Budget, and Financing –** What are your sales expectations and what amount do you need to make the budget, etc.

10. **Milestone –** The milestones are highly connected to your budget; what are the growth parameters that you expect to hit, what financial gain do you see, customer acquisitions, etc.

11. **Exit Strategy –** Any VC would like to know how much they could make, since they are in business to generate multiple returns for their investors. Have an exit strategy, like "These competitors could buy us," or "we will create a business that we wish to take public," etc.

Great ways to raise money are to visit AngelList (www.Angel.co) or apply to the big incubators, as they will assist you in the process.

Part 7

Why some people just "get it"

"A winner is a special breed, either you got it or you don't – if you didn't realize your potential yet it is time to do so!"

- Jesper Qvist, 2011

Winners have some things in common: first of all they never give up, and they are very specific in what they want, as described in the first part of this book. Taking examples of Richard Branson, Steve Jobs, Marc Zuckerberg, and Bill Gates, to name a few, you'll notice that all are visionaries that saw how their products could shape the world in the long run, and they believed in one idea solely. They did not try to start numerous companies at the same time, neither did they try to take huge unecessary risks that could harm and kill the company. Being an entrepreneur is all about your knowledge, your idea, and hiring the right people around you, and this is what made a difference for the above-mentioned entrepreneurs.

Richard Branson loved music but he didn't know much about forecasting what would sell in the future. Instead, he was good at delegating that part to a trusted friend that he employed. Nick Powel, whom Richard hired, was the one who signed the big bands and told Richard who would be great for Virgin Records in the early days. Getting the right talent on board is what got these people as far as they got in their life, and working hard made them all winners. Warren Buffet is a great example: he is supposed to be the "oracle from Omaha." If he was such a great businessman why would he lose around $100 million a year from a parent company called Net Jets, for about 10 years in a row? Many people do not ask that question but without a doubt this division is the most important and valuable asset of Berkshire Hathaway, which many people do not know. You might ask your self why? Well the answer is quite easy and frankly what matters when you invest is *information* that others do not have, but yet again it is not inside information either but legal information that Berkshire Hathaway can trade from. Net Jets serves the majority of the private aviation world (Private Jets) and they serve a major amount of the American business world with jet services or fractional ownerships. So when a company flies more than one time to the closest airport of Wal-Mart, which in Branson, the Springfield-Branson Regional Airport. Buffet's people know who is flying to that destination, so they would know right away that if a jet is chartered to a location for second time, there should be a deal and they should move in and buy the stock. Buffet and Berkshire Hathaway also often get indications from Net Jets of upcoming mergers in the stock market: if keys players in an industry keep going to a destination where a competitor is located, this could very easily indicate that a merger or hostile takeover is in progress. So the reason why Buffet has been a winner is more due to the information Net Jets provided him with, and the yearly $100 million loss is nothing compared to the money he can potentially make of the earnings in the stock market, thanks to the information acquired. So this leads us to another step: winners tend to be surrounded by more information and talented people more than others, and this is a reason why they can act as they do and keep winning in their investments.

Cases from Winners

Take a person like Jack Dorsey, Co-Founder of Twitter and relative newcomer in the scene of well-known entrepreneurs. Jack is known for his extreme focus on design and simplicity which he finds more important than anything else. Jack co-founded Twitter and later decided when he felt the company was mature enough to jump on his next venture, "Square," which is probably even more disruptive than Twitter in a sense. Twitter disrupted real-time news and thanks to that, Jack could quickly raise capital to fund his next venture, due to his newly established track record and recognition of his talent. Square is disrupting the way small stores, services, events, charity events, etc. can accept credit/debit cards. Square has simply built a small device you add to your iPhone or Android smart phone. With their software anyone would be able to accept debit/credit card payments on the phone by simply swiping the card and letting the cardholder sign on the touchscreen. This disrupts the way cards were processed before, since all you need is the phone, and Square sends the reader to you for free, which means since everyone today has a smartphone, you have no cost adding debit/credit cards to any business. Furthermore, the merchants do not pay any form for membership fee but simply just pay 2.75% in transaction fees to Square who handles everything and transfer the money to your account. So going from building a billion dollar company like Twitter to creating a disrupter in card processing is very unique. After Twitter got success, Jack Dorsey had the financial freedom to start up something without thinking about the financial part like when he started Twitter. The thing that he had as an advantage was clearly the way he thinks and sees the world as a winner, and that unique set of DNA that a winner possesses! Jack probably tried to walk into a small coffee store and realized he couldn't pay with his debit/credit card, and when asking the store owner the reply would often be the equipment is too expensive for us. So that identifies a problem as VCs expect to see when you pitch to them for capital. Secondly, Jack had information from Twitter about Android and iPhone development and their stores, since Apple and Google would like to have Twitter in the App Stores when they initially opened, and so that information was most likely shared with Twitter at an early stage. This information could be used with the problem he discovered while paying, leading him to say, "Hey, Apple and Google are creating an app store; let me create a device that accepts credit cards on a smartphone." Funding should not be a problem since Jack could present a real life problem and then a solution to it for a billion dollar market that no one really tapped into. So the whole methodology of thinking and doing things the way Jack did is a typical case of a winner that works hard and has funded two billion values companies.

Next we can take a look at the extremely hyped company Zynga, which was founded by Mark Pincus, an entrepreneur that failed several times but never quit trying. This is another characteristic of a winner, since this personality keeps trying and never gives up. Mark tried to found several companies but he never got the success that he wanted. This is obviously a problem when pitching to VCs – he never made it why would he succeed this time? (This is one of the questions that VCs will ask themselves before investing!) First Mark saw an opportunity in an unexplored market, which was to create a mass-market distribution of simple games on Facebook.

Zynga was never unique in any way, since most of their games were copied—according to lawsuits filed against the company—but they were better than others at adapting games and distribute them. But how come Zynga created a valuation of around $10 billion before they officially started trading on the stock market? First of all they got more than 250 million players in their games, but then again Electronic Arts is on the other hand "only" worth $5 billion and creates "real" games that people pay real money for to generate real revenues. So one could ask, are these high evaluations real and is Zynga worth the money? My take on it, is that Zynga has a strong user base, but their true value is way overrated, though reality down the road will show. At the end of the day the reason why Mark could raise all the money for Zynga was his small selective network that helped him, and he didn't like others focus on building a giant network of people that truly do not matter. When Zynga first took off and got many players into their games—and revenues the valuations in tech companies tend to rise a lot—Mark and the seed investors benefited highly, and later on the VCs would fight for a piece.

Promotion and Advertising

Promotion and advertising for winners are often, seen differently than others sees it. Winners tend to be masterminds of word-of-mouth advertising, and the reason why, is that their products or services are unique and disruptive in their own way. Building a strategy for aspiring startups to reach mass market with little money is always a challenge. Companies such as Mint.com, which was sold to Intuit for around $170 million less than 2 years after the company took off, is another great example of the word-of-mouth design that you should adopt. Mint tried to do many things to acquire attention in the press, but what truly made a difference was visual showings of their products, which the press and blogs loved to showcase and use for their users. Making illustrations that look cool and inform people is a very powerful tool, and tends to go viral more often than a regular press release does. Visual.ly is a great example of a company that has realized the need for buzz and creation of accurate visualization of companies, products, and services. Another tool is as described to make a product viral and give it its own life, for creating awareness and buzz. Spotify (Like iTunes, but instead you just rent music) are among many of the services that have launched in the U.S. under the basics for viral production of a product. This didn't even give them a lot of buzz and attention, but also people who didn't want to wait could pay their way in, which created a successful launch. Winners know how to analyze data and utilize the information that a user provides to them. If your website is optimized with proper analytics, it is easy to set it up so you can monetize everything and if you do promotion through Google Adwords, Facebook advertising, etc. you might be better of monetizing everything, otherwise you might not have any idea about the return on investment. Winners are people who are great at getting the most for their resources, and that is why they have become the ones they are.

Part 8

Lifestyle design

"Your time is limited, so don't waste it living someone else's life"

- Steve Jobs, Founder of Apple Inc.

Some people design their lives to become winners and they do things others just keep dreaming about. But most of these methods are possible if you are ready for change and create a lifestyle design suitable for your dreams. If you wish to live a life traveling the world, your focus for your future income is without a doubt in technology. Owning a technology company is probably the best way to be able to work form anywhere, as is becoming an author and writing a few books a year. Designing your life to travel and create incomes while working less is a challenge but a beautiful art.

Self-Publishing (Books)

Lets look at self-publishing as an author. If you first publish something and you create traction, it is basically like an annuity and here is why!

Self-publishing is all automated today; if you bought this book then the way it was produced was by print on demand (POD), so I do not need to have a publishing deal with a publishing house taking all the royalty payments. Secondly, I do not need to invest in inventory since the book is printed when you order it and print it. So that part is so simple and basic; you "*just*" have to write and market a book. Kindle and Nook are two great examples for publishing. When you publish and people buy books on the Kindle or Nook, the book is electronically delivered and you will receive between 65%-70% of the sale, which creates an interesting model, since you would be able to travel around while your books are generating income for you. Here are some sites that do print on demand and are very reasonable:

1. **CreateSpace.com** (Amazon company)

2. **Lulu.com** (If you want to make more when selling to Barnes & Noble and printing on demand as well)

3. **kdp.amazon.com** (Self-publish on the kindle)

4. **pubit.barnesandnoble.com** (Self-publish on the Nook)

5. **itunesconnect.apple.com** (When you want to publish on iBook and the iPad)

6. **Books.google.com** (Sell through Google's e-book service and get exposure online through their tools as well)

7. **Smashword.com** (E-book publisher)

The above links give you five markets plus many more that you can self-publish your book through; all you need is to buy your own ISBN number to control the publishing, and this can be done from Lulu or CreateSpace and cost around $100.

Create Apps for Mobile Devices

Being a developer of applications for smartphones such as iPhone (iOS), or for platforms like Android and Windows Mobile, is the next step for creating an income while living like a winner and traveling around the world. Selling apps to the hundreds of millions of smartphone owners out there is your potential market. This market has been shown to be highly lucrative for a business, and it is one that does not require you to work 24/7. Making apps and selling them can be extremely profitable without making a new

Angry Birds hit. Angry Birds did sell way over 200 million copies of their game at an average of $0.99, and they keep 70% of this amount so it made well over $140 million in income. But smaller apps selling around a million copies are very likely to create if you are truly unique and original. Imagine investing between $1–3,000 in an App that starts selling itself over time. What you need to do is to upload the app, create a marketing plan and have a developer create it for you. This is one of the mechanisms that winners have identified and realized how to capitalize on. Creating the App does not mean you learn how to program—though if you wish to do it yourself there are some great tools out there. For example, Ansca Mobile and Gamesalad are tools that have made it much easier for people to make their own applications for iOS and Android. Creating apps can also mean free apps with advertising in them; this creates great revenue in the long run since people tend to open the apps that show data they need on the go etc. So free apps and apps that users pay for can both be highly profitable and a method to create wealth and freedom as a winner. If you have no skills in programming and wish to hire a programmer, these are available from $10 an hour to roughly $40 an hour depending on their level. Hiring programmers on demand is easy and all you have to do is to post your job on sites like oDesk.com or Elance.com. If you do have a truly unique concept, make sure to create an NDA and have them sign it before you release all information. But as you can see, the metrics for Apps are amazing and it is a part of a lifestyle design investment that allows you to create wealth with minimum work.

Tools:

1. **www.gamesalad.com** (engine for app development like Ansca)

2. **www.anscamobile.com (**over 20 million their apps have been sold in a seven-month period)

3. **www.Android.com** (Sell and Develop)

4. **http://developer.apple.com** (sell your iPhone apps here)

5. **www.microsoft.com/windowsphone** (Sell apps here)

6. **www.amazon.com/mobile-apps** (Sell your apps here for Android)

Travel the World and Live Like a Winner!

Is working in corporate companies really worth the stress and the regular pay? What is 80 hours a week and $200,000 a year really worth for you, if you pay too much for your living standard and you do not have time to enjoy what you do and things you really value? Those are the true questions that make people rethink what's possible. If you could travel the world, if you could have more time to sail, play golf or do what interests you, would that make you a happier person? Rethink how you live and who you are; winners are never afraid of the unknown and they do take calculated chances!

Travelling the world and living in luxury is closer than you ever thought about. Let's say your rental budget in your home country is $2,000 a month, which is on a daily basis $67. If you think about quitting your regular life to travel around the world, it might be closer a dream than you ever thought it would be. Imagine traveling to countries where the economy gives you way more for your money and you can live for less than $20 a day in luxury. There are many places on earth where a lunch does not cost more than $1-2 if you want something very nice, and where the cost of living is unbelievably low!

Well first if you decide to go virtual with your life, tools such as Earthclassmail.com allows you to get a virtual mail address for your physical post and they even deposit checks you might receive to your bank account. So having access to all your physical mail online is a start—you suddenly have an address and you can live virtually any place in the world. When you've fixed that problem, and you have created a lifestyle income as a publisher or app developer, you would be able to travel and live in any place, as long as it is cheaper than your current place. This allows you to explore the world and yet make you ubiquitous. Imagine every time you have time to answer mails to people and do a social media update, you would be in a new, exotic place. This would for many portray you as a winner, and people will give you the attention that you always dreamed about.

Part 9

What are the Dangers?

"Question the unquestionable"

- Ratan Tata, Founder, Tata Group

The dangers for winners are many and the pitfalls that you can hit on the journey are even bigger in numbers. The problem is that most entrepreneurs think that they can create the next Google overnight, and when they see an internet company having success and the founders made billions, they tend to believe they can do that. This gratification of what people think they can achieve overnight is a problem, since many would tend to believe that they could become winners tomorrow. Entrepreneurship is great and we cannot advertise it enough, but being realistic and entrepreneurial at the same time is the most important. Incubators are a few of the "organs" who actually advertise and help entrepreneurs grow into winners, and these are often very important, but they can also have a negative effect if they at first do not understand your idea.

People who become winners and grow rich tend to spend money often without thinking twice. Morten Lund from Denmark, the first investor in Skype, made a killing on the sale to Ebay. He became very rich overnight and famous in the startup world. Morten started to invest in about 80-90 startups, some of which were impressive, and his network of startups was valuable. One day Morten thought he basically could walk on water since he decided to buy a free published newspaper in Denmark. This newspaper was spending money like the U.S. government. The problem was that Morten went blindly in the project and thought he could turn it around, which he came close to. But at one time Morten signed a personal liability for a loan, and when the newspaper ran out of money, so did Morten, and he lost everything. This is one of the dangers when you stop worrying and believe everything is perfect: that's when you can become dangerous for yourself. Luckily for Morten he is out of his bankruptcy today and he is running two inspiring startups: Tradeshift, which is a free invoicing platform, and Everbread, which will transform the way we book flight tickets in the near future. So the danger is always there when you start to take on too many projects and you stop seeing the disadvantages in the situations. What differentiates a true winner from the regular person is learning from one's mistakes and building on from that stage.

The Pitfalls of the New Rich

Many newly rich people tend to change behavior and habits—this is for some amazing and for others something to be aware of. Changing your lifestyle as a winner can often be challenging since you get offered so many temptations that people normally do not offer you.

Often a pitfall that people run into when starting their companies is taking on a partner. Is it good or bad – do you have the same skills or do you complement each other in different areas? The questions are many and the balance and trust is important. Often great entrepreneurs start companies with friends, family, etc. but at some point they run into a problem, and their business partners do not work as much or are focusing on other tasks. What do you do? Situations like these are common and hard to handle. Twitter is an example of a startup that in the press that seems to have the three founders coming back and forth to run the company while doing other projects. It also seems that when one has success with a new project, the others tend to get jealous, and this is not a great picture from the outside. Other pitfalls people run into at times is starting from scratch rather than buying an under-evaluated company and building it up. Look at Wayne Huizenga: he saw the opportunity with Blockbuster, bought them since he knew they where under-evaluated and made the company the great success story they were in the late 1990s and early 2000s. If Huizenga didn't buy blockbuster but rather started from scratch, he most likely would never have had the same success. Another common pitfall that comes from the same Blockbuster transaction is that entrepreneurs need to know when the price is good, and they see a paradigm shift coming, to sell at the top like Huizenga did with Blockbuster. Keeping the company at times hoping to create a larger growth on your own is very dangerous and often what can bankrupt or destroy great entrepreneurs, since they refuse to give their baby away for a hefty bonus.

Entrepreneurs who are not winners often tend to think that their idea is the company and that is the ultimate goal. The only problem is, these personalities often tend to see people as machines and not the important talent that you need. It is often these people that make the company and not the idea, which is also why VCs often do not pay too much attention to the idea they invest in if the team is right; they know they will get it right! Secondly be realistic. Some entrepreneurs believe they can do the impossible, and yes if you have a billion dollars like Richard Branson, then you can build your own spaceship and a space travel agency called Virgin Galactic, but if you don't you need to be realistic with the money available. Remember: winners know reality, and the others might live in a fantasy world.

Do not think too small. It is better to make part of a goal that is too big, rather than accomplishing a small goal. Imagine your goal is to open a Subway franchise and buy a certain house and car. What happens the second you accomplish that—are you happy, or should you have set your goal higher? As Michelangelo quoted:

"The greater danger for most of us lies not in setting our aim too high and falling short; but in setting our aim too low, and achieving our mark"

So the ones that think too small, would never become a winner!

Entrepreneurs often tend to hire cheap employees, as I warned against in outsourcing experiences. Hiring cheap people does often create more problems down the road and as most people know cheap people end up paying twice. So never underpay employees; they will perform better when paid well and when you support their beliefs and work.

Entrepreneurs often forget to protect themselves and their intellectual property. Patents, trademark and copyright are extremely important in protecting the work a winner has done, and they know that. There are companies that fully live on their patents and license them to others. For example in the pharmaceutical industry, you often see the small laboratory that developed a new medicine often gets acquired for a big million dollar price tag. This is often for the pharmaceutical company to gain new revenue sources and keep the competition out. IP is a valuable asset, as well: see Microsoft every time a person buys an Android HTC phone. It is estimated that HTC pays Microsoft a patent royalty of $10 per handset sold. This is a gigantic revenue source that they secured by thinking like a winner!

Finally, a good business or entrepreneur will always deliver what it promises, but a great business will deliver more than promised. This is really what makes the difference between a winner and the rest!

Part 10

Everyone has a winner's DNA!

"Winning is the most important. Everything is consequence of that."

\- Ayrton Senna, Formula-1 World Champion

Everybody has a chance in life, and if the person really wants something, that person can become a winner like anyone else. Some people might have a "born" gift to do it more easily than others but at the end of the day the talent can be achievable for anyone if they really care. Applying the knowledge from this book and thinking positively in life are, the first steps toward becoming a winner. It is not how we are born, nor the DNA that is in our bodies, but the knowledge and curiosity we observe down the road in our lives that really matters. Creating a business that matters and doing what you love is often what makes the difference between failure and joining the winners. This is from the simple fact that if you love what you do, you work harder, but also feel fine delegating projects to others; that is what really is characteristic of a winner. Thinking about what it takes is all about knowing yourself and to which direction you can push your own limits in a great way.

Do you have what it takes?

The real question you can ask you self is: do I have what it takes to be a winner and create products that can make money during my absence and contradict the talk about hard work?

These are a few illustrations of companies and income revenue you can make in absence, which creates wealth a new way that didn't exist five years ago. Imagining spending some time creating a product, such an app or a book, and then marketing it a few hours a week, so that you can spend the rest of the time traveling the world and enjoying life. This is some common trait of winners, and others are the ones that fight for venture capital and create huge companies, but that is demanding and requires a greater amount of effort and time. So the real question is, when you have different choices which one do you pick, to be the winner with all the time in the world, or be the winner that works hard and becomes even richer?

No matter what choice you make, the decision and opportunity is there. If you know everything about cutting flowers or have a great imagination, why not to express it to others through a book? It is not that difficult to self-publish, as I've showed you, nor is it expensive to find a copy editor to make sure your material is perfect. So if you believe that you have a story or information you want to share, create a book or online webcasts and sell your knowledge to others. That way, you will generate revenue and down the road become a winner. If you love to work hard and have your fingers on the pulse on what happening on a daily basis in the world, and love to be entrepreneurial, go out give it a try. Crowdsource your ideas to shape them, like this book cover is crowdsourced. Get help from others, find a great team filled with talent and go get some capital. It is all about the effort you are willing to bring into any project, since all the tools are available pretty much for free today.

Understand the Steps

You need to know that crowdsourcing is more powerful than most people tend to believe. I have a friend who has published four books now, and I told him to Crowdsource the cover design. He used to pay between around $1200-1500 for cover designs, and now he realized that he can get more choices and ideas for as little as $200 for the same product. So understanding the use of a crowd is paramount in order to achieve status as a winner. Secondly, don't give up on understanding technology; it is a must, and it provides much more value than you would believe. Small changes on the technological front can often lead to an increase of thousands of dollars in revenue, instantly. Third, talent, talent, talent—you need to find it and bring the right people on board, whether for sales, creativity, development, or to get your business up and going. Be aware of your planning. It is important to try and create traction on what you do, but if you want to make the product viral you might not want to unleash it without doing a slow beta release to create awareness. When going live always remember your customers or potential users and listen to them, figure out why and how you provide them with more value than anyone else. Look at Virgin America and JetBlue Airlines: both provide satellite TV, bigger leather seats, free soft drinks, and other frills to compete against other airlines, and this is what you need to identify the competitive advantage you will market. Social media is not just a marketing channel but it is rather an avenue for creating awareness and being accessible to the customer, and it remains an essential tool for understanding your crowd. Grabbing attention is a part of the initial launch, as you should beware of, but focusing on analytics and optimization is the most important factor when you first get customers in. As described, analytics can bring you revenue gain of 30%-500%, sometimes from small changes, and this is truly something anyone can feel.

But at the end of the day, figure out how you want to live your life and build your business around that ideology!

Starting your own business is fun, easy, and challenging, so get out there and give it a try—you might learn something and hopefully follow my advices to become a winner!

Bonus Part 11

Entrepreneurial Myths!

"When you are winning a war almost everything that happens can be claimed to be right and wise."

- Winston Churchill

Myth 1: Entrepreneurs are like top athletes: they are born, not made.

This is not true. Research has shown that entrepreneurial parents raised only a small percentage of entrepreneurs who are successful today. But the most successful entrepreneurs revealed that 52 percent were the first in their immediate families to start a business, which might seem surprising when we talk about personalities such as Bill Gates (Microsoft), Jeff Bezos (Amazon), Larry Page (Google), and Sergey Brin (Google), who all became billionaires. Their parents were academics, lawyers, factory workers, or bureaucrats. This is a clear example of great entrepreneurs that have made a difference for everybody's life, yet were not born with the DNA.

Myth 2: College dropouts make for better entrepreneurs

Overall, we all hear the stories about dropouts like Mark Zuckerberg, Bill Gates, and Richard Branson, who all made it to the list of winning billionaires. But is the "lack" of education what made them brilliant and so successful? Research has proven that being a dropout does not make you a better entrepreneur—in fact, having a higher education will prepare you better for entrepreneurship. Bill Gates and Mark Zuckerberg might have been college dropouts, but they still attended college. They might never have graduated, but that does not mean they didn't learn anything in school. On average, companies founded by college graduates have twice the sales and workforce of companies founded by people who didn't go to college, which should indicate a difference between them. What is surprising to some people is the fact that graduation from an elite university does not prove to be any advantage at all in entrepreneurship.

Myth 3: The typical tech entrepreneurs are in their 20s or early 30s.

There is proven advantage in technology by being younger, since you tend to better understand the overall meaning of concepts and methodologies behind technology. Being younger also makes you willing to disrupt and influence things to your way. What actually is the case with most entrepreneurs is the fact that they get tired of working for someone else, and they wish to create their own parameters for their life. It is not true that most entrepreneurs are young: in fact Jeff Bezos was not a young man when he founded Amazon, and Reed Hastings was not young when he founded Netflix. So being young might give you an adaptability advantage, but experience-wise you might lack from others that close circle of friends in his or hers network that can create true value.

Myth 4: Most entrepreneurs are motivated by fame and money.

This is not true; in fact, most entrepreneurs believe only in their idea, and that is really all that matters. They are motivated by the desire to work for themselves, and being able to work anywhere and anytime. They like to solve problems, create value and products. The money is just a bonus, and I bet if you told someone you are founding a company just for the money, they would assume that you will fail right away.

Myth 5: You need venture capital to succeed and foster innovation

False. Venture capital is only raised when you need it, for the simple reason that you as the owner need to give away equity of your company and power to access the capital. If you want growth higher than the organic growth that your company can create, then yes, venture capital is a great idea for a few reasons: they provide you with a network and financial stability to concentrate on developing and creating more market traction for your product. Another bonus when you attract venture capital is that your company is often valuated more highly, since VCs do not want to deal with companies less than $3-10 million in market value. Venture capital is not necessary to create growth, but it is a great tool to raise more capital, gain great exposure in the press, and provide stability for you and your employees.

Myth 6: It takes a lot of money to start a business

Money is not the main concern it all depends on your industry, idea, and product is developing and creating a company cheaper than ever before. If you follow the steps of this book and use tools to crowdsource and outsource your idea, it might be cheaper and more realistic to start the business you always dreamed about. Web development used to be expensive, but now you can access great talent for $10-15 an hour, which might cost $200-300 an hour in the U.S.

Index

Definitions

Angel investor: is the first person after friends or family that will invest in you startup, and this person is often extremely important in shaping you and your companies future.

Acquisition/Acquire: is when you get a new customer (the value it cost to obtain the new customer)

Beta: the stage when a product is still classified as "in development," in the late stages.

Blue Ocean Strategy: there are red and blue oceans, which describes the universe of a market. *Red Oceans* are all the industries in existence today—the known market space. *Blue oceans*, in contrast, denote all the industries not in existence today—the unknown market space, untainted by competition

Crowdsourcing: an open call to a group of people that solves a problem for you.

Crowdfunding: a group of people pays money together to help the person to raise the money he or she is asking for.

Crowd-casting: when a group of people vote and create ideas for you.

Crowd-creation: when the crowd solves a problem for you.

Deck: a PowerPoint presentation that shows your concept or idea. It includes sections such as: Like problem, solution to it, financial and marketing.

Innovation: invention + commercialization = Innovation

Incubator: "one-stop" delivery of business support services for new firms, often linked to a university or a large public research institution—traditionally, the package includes inexpensive accommodation, but virtual incubation is becoming more common.

Initial Public Offering (IPO): the "flotation" of a company through the open sale of its shares in a stock market—the conventional exit route for early investors such as *business angels and venture capital* funds.

Landing page: is the page that you first see when you search or come to a website, so a landing page is the first view a customer has a your business, might be your only shot to sell!

Outsourcing: hiring an individual or a company to perform tasks outside the company, often done because the price is lower.

Seed Capital: seed capital funds invest relatively small sums in *startups* at the earliest stage, often to finance feasibility and market studies. Many universities and large companies have established dedicated seed funds to stimulate spin-off activity.

Startup: a newly formed company

Venture Capital: high-risk, high-return investment. Venture capital funds are essential as a means of financing the rapid growth of new technology-based firms.

Winner: a champion, or the person who is the best in their respective field.

About the Author

A highly educated *winner* with an MBA in Management from Nova Southeastern University and a Master of Science in Management of Innovation and Business Development from Copenhagen Business School.

Jesper Qvist is an accomplished entrepreneur with a huge knowledge base about entrepreneurship and strategy, which he is sharing in his first book, *A Winners DNA*. Jesper is originally from Denmark but lives in Miami Beach, Florida. He is also the founder of Voogy.com – the first real print market in the U.S.

Twitter: @Jqvist

Web: www.AWinnersDNA.com

www.JesperQvist.com

www.Voogy.com

Notes

www.ingramcontent.com/pod-product-compliance
Lightning Source LLC
Chambersburg PA
CBHW032003190326
41520CB00007B/336